best hikes with dogs

TEXAS HILL COUNTRY AND COAST

CONTENTS

Acknowledgments 12

Part 1: Hiking With Your Dog

Good Dogs Require Good Owners 14
Health Concerns for Your Dog 17
Wildlife 19
Permits and Regulations 24
Go Lightly on the Land 26
Myths and Misunderstandings about Dogs 27
Gear for You and Your Dog 29
Camp Care: Cleanup 33
Safety 33
Weather 34
Using This Book 38
How the Trails Were Selected 39
Enjoy the Trails: Get Involved 39

Part 2: The Trails

Austin

1. Emma Long Metropolitan Park, Turkey Creek Trail 42
2. Barton Creek Greenbelt 45
3. Bull Creek Greenbelt Trail 48
4. Southeast Metropolitan Park, Primitive Trail 52
5. Richard Moya Park 55

Highland Lakes

6. Pace Bend County Park 58
7. Grelle Recreation Area 61
8. Muleshoe Bend Recreation Area 64
9. Arkansas Bend Park 67
10. Inks Lake State Park 70
11. Canyon of the Eagles, Peacock and Juniper Ridge Loops 73
12. Canyon of the Eagles, Beebrush, Live Oak, and Vireo Hill Trails 76
13. Canyon of the Eagles, Lakeside Trail 79

Austin Low Country

14. Lake Georgetown, Good Water Trail   82
15. Bastrop State Park, Lost Pines Trail   88
16. Lake Bastrop South Shore Park   91
17. Buescher State Park   93
18. McKinney Falls State Park, Homestead Trail   98
19. McKinney Roughs Nature Park, Outer Loop   101
20. McKinney Roughs Nature Park, Woodland and Bluff
    Ridge Trails   104
21. Lake Somerville State Park and Trailway   107

San Antonio

22. O. P. Schnabel Park, Leon Creek Vista   111
23. Eisenhower Park, Yucca and Hill View Trails   114
24. Cibolo Nature Center   117
25. Medina River Park, Rio Medina Trail   120
26. Government Canyon State Natural Area, Lytle's Loop   124
27. Palmetto State Park   127

Hill Country

28. Pedernales Falls State Park, Wolf Mountain Trail   131
29. Guadalupe River State Park, Loop Trails   134
30. Colorado Bend State Park, Spicewood Springs Trail   138
31. Enchanted Rock State Natural Area, Loop Trail   142
32. Enchanted Rock State Natural Area, Echo Canyon Trail   145
33. Hill Country State Natural Area, Loop to
    Wilderness Camp   148
34. Hill Country State Natural Area, Comanche Bluff Trail   152
35. Lost Maples State Natural Area, East Trail   156
36. South Llano River State Park, Fawn Trail   160
37. South Llano River State Park, Wildlife Management
    Area Trail   164
38. Lake Brownwood State Park, Texas Oak Trail   168

Gulf Coast

39. Memorial Park, Purple Trail   172
40. George Bush Park, Equestrian Center to Sports Park   176
41. Lake Houston State Park, North River Trail   178
42. Lake Livingston State Park   182
43. Lake Texana State Park, Trailhead 2   186
44. Huntsville State Park   188
45. Brazos Bend State Park, Elm and 40-Acre Lake Trails   191
46. Big Thicket National Preserve, Sundew Trail   195
47. Big Thicket National Preserve, Woodlands Trail   198
48. Sam Houston National Forest, Lone Star Hiking Trail   202

The Shore

49. Crystal Beach   207
50. Galveston Island State Park, Bayou Trails   209
51. Brazoria National Wildlife Refuge, Big Slough Trail   213
52. Padre Island National Seashore   216
53. Matagorda Island Wildlife Management Area   219
54. Aransas National Wildlife Refuge, Dagger Point Trail   223
55. Matagorda County Beach   226

   Resources   231
   Index   233

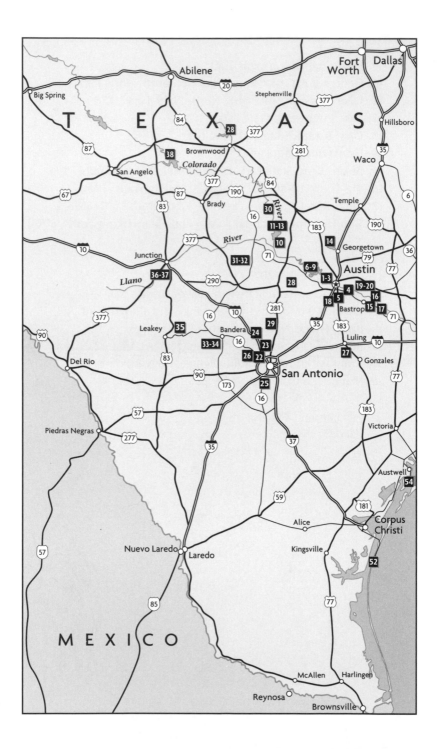

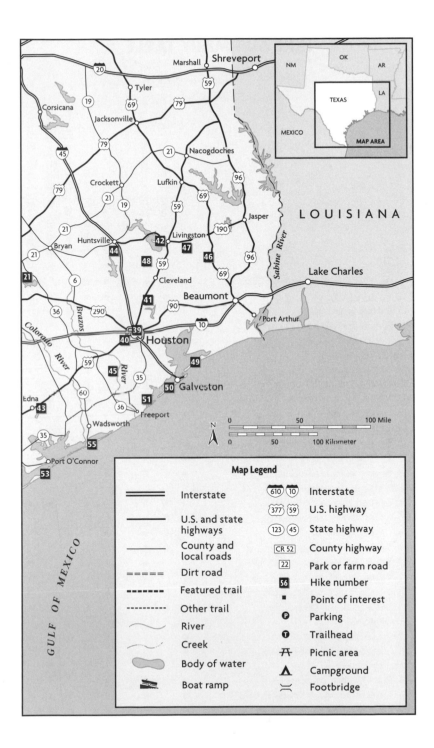

HIKE SUMMARY TABLE

Hike	Up to 5 miles	More than 5 miles (C) = camping	Water (S) = seasonal	Unleashed okay	Mostly shady	Best for fit dogs	Good for older/less fit dogs	Shorter distance possible	Share with horses/bikes
Austin									
1. Emma Long Metropolitan Park, Turkey Creek Trail	●		●	●	●	●			
2. Barton Creek Greenbelt		●	●		●	●		●	●
3. Bull Creek Greenbelt Trail	●		●		●		●	●	
4. Southeast Metropolitan Park Primitive Trail	●		●			●			
5. Richard Moya Park	●				●		●	●	
Highland Lakes									
6. Pace Bend County Park	●		●	●	●	●			●
7. Grelle Recreation Area	●		S	●	●	●			
8. Muleshoe Bend Recreation Area		●	●	●		●		●	
9. Arkansas Bend Park	●		●			●			
10. Inks Lake State Park	●		●			●			
11. Canyon of the Eagles, Peacock/Juniper Ridge Loops	●				●	●			
12. Canyon of the Eagles, Beebrush/Live Oak/Vireo Hill Trails	●						●		
13. Canyon of the Eagles, Lakeside Trail	●		●		●		●		
Austin Low Country									
14. Lake Georgetown, Good Water Trail		C	●				●	●	●
15. Bastrop State Park, Lost Pines Trail		C	S		●	●			
16. Lake Bastrop/South Shore Park	●		●		●		●		
17. Buescher State Park		●	S		●	●		●	
18. McKinney Falls State Park, Homestead Trail	●		●		●	●			●
19. McKinney Roughs Nature Park, Outer Loop	●		●		●	●		●	●
20. McKinney Roughs Nature Park, Woodland/Bluff Ridge Trails	●				●	●			
21. Lake Somerville State Park and Trailway		C	●			●		●	●
San Antonio									
22. O. P. Schnabel Park, Leon Creek Vista	●				●			●	●
23. Eisenhower Park, Yucca/Hill View Trails	●					●			
24. Cibolo Nature Center	●		●			●		●	
25. Medina River Park, Rio Medina Trail	●		●		●	●			
26. Government Canyon State Natural Area, Lytle's Loop	●		S		●				●
27. Palmetto State Park	●		●		●		●	●	

Hike	Up to 5 miles	More than 5 miles (C) = camping	Water (S) = seasonal	Unleashed okay	Mostly shady	Best for fit dogs	Good for older/less fit dogs	Shorter distance possible	Share with horses/bikes
Hill Country									
28. Pedernales Falls State Park, Wolf Mountain Trail		●	●		●	●			
29. Guadalupe River State Park, Loop Trails		●				●		●	●
30. Colorado Bend Spicewood Springs Trail		●	●		●	●		●	
31. Enchanted Rock State Natural Area, Loop Trail	●		●			●			
32. Enchanted Rock State Natural Area, Echo Canyon Trail	●		S			●			
33. Hill Country State Natural Area, Wilderness Camp Trail		●	●			●		●	●
34. Hill Country State Natural Area, Comanche Bluff Trail	●	●	●			●		●	●
35. Lost Maples State Natural Area, East Trail	●		●			●			
36. South Llano River State Park, Fawn Trail	●		S			●			
37. South Llano River State Park, Wildlife Management Area Trail		●				●			●
38. Lake Brownwood State Park, Texas Oak Trail	●		●		●	●			
Gulf Coast									
39. Memorial Park, Purple Trail	●		S		●		●		●
40. George Bush Park, Equestrian Center to Sports Park		●					●		
41. Lake Houston State Park, North River Trail		●	●		●	●		●	●
42. Lake Livingston State Park	●		●		●	●	●	●	
43. Lake Texana State Park, Trailhead 2	●		●		●	●	●	●	
44. Hunstville State Park		C	S		●	●			
45. Brazos Bend State Park, Elm/40-Acre Lake Trails	●		●			●	●	●	
46. Big Thicket National Preserve, Sundew Trail	●				●		●	●	
47. Big Thicket National Preserve, Woodlands Trail		●			●		●	●	
48. Sam Houston National Forest, Lone Star Hiking Trail		C	●		●		●	●	
The Shore									
49. Crystal Beach	●							●	●
50. Galveston Island State Park, Bayou Trails	●		●		●	●			
51. Brazoria NWR, Big Slough Trail	●					●		●	
52. Padre Island National Seashore		C				●		●	
53. Matagorda Island Wildlife Management Area		C				●		●	
54. Aransas National Wildlife Refuge, Dagger Point Trail	●				●			●	●
55. Matagorda County Beach		●		●				●	●

ACKNOWLEDGMENTS

Thanks to my family—my husband, Corey, and children, Holly, Collin, and Bridget—for supporting my hiking habit and occasionally joining me. Thanks to hiker Elaine Osmun, Dr. Lore Haug and the Texas A&M University College of Veterinary Medicine and Biomedical Sciences, and Bill Read at the National Weather Service for sharing their expertise in various areas, and to all of the park staff who helped me find my way around and checked my work. And, of course, thanks to Max and Keeper, my four-legged trail buddies.

PART I

Hiking with Your Dog

Texas is a great place to enjoy the outdoors, from the steep granite of Enchanted Rock to the smooth, flat shores of the Gulf, and hiking is one of the best and most versatile outdoor activities. An enjoyable way to hike is with a four-legged friend; your dog gets to hark back to his wild roots, you get a near-ideal hiking companion, and you both get some fresh air and healthy exercise. Exercise is not only important for your dog's physical health; it also helps keep him from becoming bored, which can lead to bad behavior. This guide will help you get ready to hit the trail with your dog, offer guidance on being a safe and considerate hiker, and point you to some of the best hikes convenient to Austin, San Antonio, and Houston.

Nature is a dynamic system, not an exhibit in a museum, and as such is always changing. Trees fall, streams dry up or change course, rocks slide. Always contact the park office or other land manager for updates on trail conditions and current weather and forecasts. Consider the distance and difficulty of your hike and prepare accordingly—be sure you and your dog are in shape, pack adequate food and water, and allow plenty of time to finish your hike or reach a campground before dark. Pick up trail maps from state park offices or other places where indicated, or purchase the appropriate map from the United States Geological Service (USGS). Call your local vet and a vet in the area you will be hiking for the latest on any potential problems and to identify a place you can take your dog in case of emergency.

And, most important, have fun out there with your pal.

Good Dogs Require Good Owners

Just as good fences make good neighbors, good owners make for good dogs. You don't want to run into unruly or aggressive dogs on the trail, and neither does anyone else.

Control Your Dog

Before you hoist your backpack and snap on the leash, a basic obedience course—whether self-taught or from a professional—is a must. Just because you'll be in the great outdoors doesn't mean you won't need to count on your dog to come when called or stay when commanded. In fact, in some places, that obedience will be critical to the safety of your dog (think snakes and alligators), or of wildlife such as turtles, deer, or birds. Public hiking trails belong to everyone, and all users are entitled to a safe and pleasant experience. An unruly or annoying dog

Lexi notices something interesting on a shady hike with Debbie in Huntsville State Park.

can make other visitors think that canines should be barred from parks and trails—and those of us who enjoy getting out with our dogs don't want that to happen.

Socialization

Be sure your dog is socialized to people and other dogs. You can accomplish this by exposing him to both from an early age, either informally or formally through a class or doggie day-care play dates. For most hiking trails, your dog also must be respectful of wild animals, from armadillos to deer, pigs, and alligators, and in some places, he'll need to be cool with horses, too. If you're in doubt, don't strike out on a 7-mile hike only to realize 5 miles down the trail that your dog goes berserk when encountering any of those animals. Find a controlled situation with a quick exit where you can expose your dog to others. If you continue to have problems with your dog's reactions, seek out a professional trainer experienced with this problem.

Good Canine Trail Etiquette

A few simple rules will help you and your dog have a good hiking experience—and ensure that everyone else does, too. Always stay on established trails. Hiking "off road" can damage the environment, and hazards to

you and your dog are harder to spot when you are not on a trail. Sometimes there are trails leading off the official one that have been created by many feet leaving the established path. Try to avoid these, as your feet will contribute to the problem, and you may end up lost as well. Yield to horses and uphill travelers. If you are hiking with friends, walk single file when approaching other trail users. Do not approach or disturb wildlife, and do not feed wild animals. Keep your dog on leash where required.

Finally, always, always scoop the poop. Dog feces are not a part of the natural environment. In fact, according to a 1999 Vanderbilt University study, canine fecal matter is a major cause of water pollution in urban and suburban areas. The Texas Natural Resource Conservation Commission estimates that dogs leave some 500,000 pounds of poop in Austin's Town Lake watershed each year, or about 1327 pounds a day. Dog waste can contain harmful bacteria and viruses, as well as nutrients that accelerate the growth of nuisance algae. An average-size dog dropping produces 3 billion fecal coliform bacteria! Rain carries doggie poop into streams and rivers, directly or through storm drains. Besides the potential harm to the environment, there is also the "eewww" factor—no one likes to step in or smell dog waste. If that isn't enough to convince you, consider that cleanup is the law in many places. The city of Austin, for example, has an ordinance requiring prompt removal of animal waste, with a potential fine for noncompliance. Carry plastic bags with you (the ones that cover your newspaper work fine, as do grocery produce bags). If you find yourself miles from a trailhead and discover that you forgot to bring bags, at the very least move your dog's handiwork from the trail and bury it.

Sierra remains on her leash while enjoying a short break on a long hike on the Good Water Trail.

Health Concerns for Your Dog

Your dog will no doubt be enthusiastic about hiking with you, and the activity should be enjoyable and healthy for both of you. There are, however, some things you need to do to prepare your dog, and a few possible health hazards to consider.

Getting in Shape

Before embarking on a hike, be sure you and your dog are both in shape. This doesn't require a fancy workout plan; the best way to get into shape is to start walking. Work your way up from short distances on level ground, about fifteen minutes or so, to longer distances and some challenges like climbing hills or getting over rocks. Most dogs in normal condition can handle a one-day hike of 10 miles, but they could get overfatigued and sore if called upon to do the same thing the next day (kind of like their owners). Work up to longer distances with your dog just as you do for yourself, although he'll probably get in shape faster. When you hike, walk slowly for the first five to ten minutes to allow your dog (and you) to warm up; if you take a strenuous hike, walk slowly for five to ten minutes at the end to cool down, too. An overweight dog should not hike because the activity may put undue stress on bones and joints and make the dog more prone to injury. If you are thinking that hiking is a way to help your pooch lose weight, consider starting with regular, short walks around the neighborhood, gradually working your way up to longer distances as he slims down.

Puppies don't have fully developed muscles and bones and should not be taken on serious hikes until at least 14 months of age. Depending on the breed, this is when growth plates on bones have mostly closed, but it can be later for larger dogs. Ask your vet if your puppy is ready to hit the trail. If yes, also remember that puppies need even more water than adult dogs do.

Tender Feet

Your dog also may need to be preconditioned to what to expect on the trail, particularly her comfort level crossing water and getting her paws wet. Although we think of dogs as outdoor animals, many have never encountered a natural pond or stream. City dogs may even need a little encouragement to drink from these natural sources the first few times.

After every hike, inspect your dog's feet to make sure there are no stickers or other foreign objects lodged between the pads, and check for injuries. If your dog does not walk on concrete or other hard surfaces often enough to keep his nails worn down, be sure to have them trimmed regularly, as walking on untrimmed nails can be painful for your dog. Trimming excess hair on your dog's feet is also a good idea, as the hair can trap moisture, dirt, and stickers and can prevent air from circulating around the pads, which helps your dog dissipate heat.

Vet Checkups

Before hitting the trail with your dog, head to the vet for a checkup to make sure there are no health issues that would preclude such activity. Once you get the all clear, be sure to update vaccination records and have ID and license tags and a heartworm preventative. Prepare for any potential health risks specific to the region where you'll be hiking. It is a good idea to contact a veterinarian in the area to ask about any issues and concerns, and to find a vet who can provide care should anything happen to your dog when you're away from home.

Heat Stroke and Sunburn

Heat stroke is a serious and common problem in Texas, even when dogs are in the shade and have plenty of drinking water. As we all know, dogs cool themselves by panting rather than sweating. A dog's normal temperature is between 100°F and 102°F, and heat stroke occurs when it reaches 109°F or higher. Overexertion is a common cause of heat stroke in dogs, and what might be normal exercise for your dog can become overexertion when the air is hot. Always carry plenty of water for both you and your dog, and take advantage of shady spots to rest in when the temperature soars. Dogs at greater risk for heat stroke include those with short noses, such as boxers and pugs, dogs with heavy coats, such as collies and chows, those who have had heat stroke before, and elderly dogs or those with health problems.

It might not be practical to take your dog's temperature on a hike, but you can test for heat stroke by lifting the dog's lip; the inner lips and gums should be pink, and the color should go from pink to white to pink again within one to two seconds when you press your finger against them. If the inner lips and gums are darker, or it takes less than one second or more than two for the color to return to pink, your dog may have heat stroke. If your dog is panting aggressively, his tongue is hanging far out and is spread wide like a soup ladle, his eyes and ears are red, and he feels warm, he is likely in heat exhaustion and headed toward heat stroke. Stop activity immediately, either by ending your hike or putting the dog on leash (if he's been off) and getting him to be still (not all dogs have the sense to stop activity on their own), and get out of the heat as quickly as possible. Cool down the dog's body by placing cool, wet towels over the head and neck, belly, and pads of the feet; placing him in a bathtub with cool (not cold) running water; or hosing him off with a garden hose. Then get your dog to a veterinarian as soon as possible to avoid complications from heat stroke. If your dog starts staggering, throws up, falls down, or doesn't want to walk, he is likely suffering from heat stroke. Treat him immediately and get to a veterinary clinic as soon as possible.

Heat can be a problem for the pads of your dog's feet, too. Check the temperature of pavement or rocks with your bare hand; if a surface is too hot to touch comfortably, it is too hot for your dog to walk on unprotected. Put on dog booties or hike in the early morning or evening.

Dogs can get sunburned, too, especially on their noses and ears, and can even get skin cancer as a result. While there are special sunscreens for dogs, the human kind works just as well as long as it is water (i.e., lick) resistant. Use an SPF 15 or higher, and apply to noses, ears, and stomachs—places with little pigment or hair. More important, stick to the shade as much as possible and avoid having Fido out in the high sun of midday.

Wildlife

You and your pooch will be sharing the great outdoors with a lot of other critters, from the benign to the downright dangerous. Knowing what you are likely to run across, and how to respond, will help keep your hikes safe and enjoyable.

Mosquitoes and Fleas

Millions of mosquitoes and other biting insects call Texas home, and some carry diseases. Mosquitoes, in particular, carry heartworm, and a preventative is essential for dogs in areas where there are mosquitoes—which is just about anywhere in the state. Heartworm preventatives are available in easy-to-give monthly doses, and some are combined with flea and tick protection. Some topical flea repellents are said to repel mosquitoes, but to be on the safe side, spray your dog with mosquito repellent when heading out on hikes in areas where these pests are likely.

While such sprays are sold over the counter, it is best to get them through your veterinarian, as some products may be toxic to dogs. Some

Hikers often encounter armadillos on Texas trails. Fortunately, the strange critters are harmless.

animals, and people, too, have a strong reaction to DEET-based mosquito repellents, and these probably should not be used on your dog. Choose a repellent designed specifically for dogs, and restrict application to those places the dog can't lick—the back of the neck and around the ears, staying well clear of the ears themselves. These are logical places that mosquitoes will be looking for exposed skin to bite. Avon has a product called Skin-So-Soft that many people swear by to repel mosquitoes, and some vets recommend it for your dog.

You can control fleas naturally with regular use of a flea comb, hot soapy water, and a vacuum cleaner. Seasoning your dog's food with brewer's yeast and garlic can also help repel fleas. Healthy pets are more resistant to fleas in general, so give your dog a food with adequate protein and limit or avoid those with additives and preservatives.

Snakes

Humans and dogs are not prey for venomous snakes; given the choice, snakes want to avoid you. Do your part by avoiding them. Stay away from or be careful around rocks and woodpiles, and don't allow your dog to stick her nose or paws in holes and crevices. Be careful when sitting down on or stepping over logs. Most important, always be on the lookout for snakes. Some dogs don't mess with snakes, or naturally move away from them, but others go looking for them. Know which type your dog is; if he's the latter, keep him close to you in places likely to have snakes (or consider snake-aversion training).

Texas is home to several types of poisonous snakes, including copperheads, cottonmouths, rattlesnakes, and coral snakes. All of these are pit vipers and can be identified by triangular heads and elliptical eye pupils. Of course, you have to get fairly close to make an identification, so your best bet is just to steer clear of all snakes. Copperheads are generally found in rocky areas and wooded bottomlands, rarely in dry areas. Cottonmouths live in the eastern half of the state in swamps and sluggish waterways, coastal marshes, rivers, ponds, and streams. They are a good reason to keep your dog out of these bodies of water. About half the poisonous snakes in Texas are rattlers, and the species you are most likely to encounter in the Hill Country and coastal areas are the prairie rattler and the western diamondback, which can reach 7 feet in length. Diamondbacks are brown with diamond-shaped markings along the middle of the back and are found in all but the easternmost part of the state. The prairie rattler is greenish or grayish with darker, rounded blotches on the back. It reaches about 3 feet in length and lives in grassy plains in the western third of the state. Contrary to the popular myth, rattlesnakes don't always rattle before striking. Coral snakes have a

A red slider crosses the trail near Sandy Creek in Enchanted Rock.

Wildflowers grace much of Texas almost year-round, but snakes like thick underbrush, so enjoy flowers from the trail.

distinctive black-, yellow-, and red-ringed pattern, with the red and yellow rings always touching. Several harmless snakes have similar markings but without this distinction. Texans all learn the saying "Red and yellow, kill a fellow; red and black, venom lack." Coral snakes live in the southeastern half of Texas in woodlands, canyons, and coastal plains.

Fortunately, about half of all venomous snakebites are dry, which means no venom is injected. If a venomous snake bites your dog and venom is injected, there will be swelling accompanied by bruising and bloody oozing. If there is no oozing, it might be a bee sting or something else. Snakebites can be fatal to dogs, depending on the type of snake, size of the dog, where the bite is, and how much venom was injected. If a dog is bitten multiple times, it is more likely that venom was injected. Treatments are available, and the likelihood of a bite being fatal is less if the dog is treated. If you think your dog has been bitten, get to a vet as soon as possible. Remember that only one or two people in Texas die from snakebites each year—low odds compared to many risks, and your dog's odds are even better.

A rattlesnake vaccine is available, however, and may be a good idea if you hike with your dog in snake territory on a regular basis. The vaccine has to be given multiple times to be effective, so start several months in advance of when your dog will need protection. This also must be done annually.

Alligators

Generally, areas where alligators live will be signed as such. Do not allow your dog in the water in these areas, not even at the edge to drink. Alligators are very fast and have been known to dine on dogs. Observe the following rules of alligator etiquette, developed by the Texas Parks and Wildlife Department.

Alligator Etiquette

- Absolutely do not feed or harass alligators. If you love your pet, keep it on a leash. Do not throw objects into the water for your dog to retrieve.
- Do not assume alligators are slow moving or sluggish.
- Keep a safe distance of at least 30 feet from an alligator at all times.
- If you hook a fish, an alligator might go after your catch.
- Avoid any alligator sunning itself in the middle of the trail.
- If you see a pile of twigs, grasses, and/or soil near the side of the trail, avoid it. It's a nest and the mother alligator is probably close by guarding it.
- When an alligator stands its ground, opens its mouth, and hisses, you have come too close.
- Plan a route of retreat. Retreat slowly and make no quick moves. Keep your eyes on the alligator. Retreat uphill where possible. Keep retreating in this manner until the alligator no longer demonstrates aggressive behavior. Above all, do not get close enough to threaten an alligator.

Poison Ivy

Dogs can get poison ivy, but they generally do not, thanks to their fur. A greater risk is that your dog will pick up the plant oils on her fur and transmit them to you. When you hike in areas with poison ivy, be sure to bathe your dog, and yourself, thoroughly after your hike. Poison ivy has compound leaves consisting of three pointed leaflets, with a longer stalk on the middle one. The leaflet edges can be smooth or toothed and vary in size, and clusters of tiny berries sometimes grow at forks in the stems. The plant can climb, creep, and look like a bush. It is reddish in spring, green in summer, and shades of yellow, orange, or red in fall. Many plants, like Virginia creeper, look similar to poison ivy. When in doubt, avoid touching the plant! People react differently, but contact typically causes a blistery rash that is very itchy and can last for days.

Over-the-counter preparations such as calamine lotion or Aveeno bath products can provide some relief from the itching.

Permits and Regulations

You will have to pay an entrance fee at most parks. Some fees are per person, while others are per vehicle. Since these fees support upkeep and maintenance in the parks, think of paying them as your contribution to keeping our outdoor spaces available for our enjoyment. Fees are subject to change, so call ahead or check park websites before heading out.

Annual Passes

An annual Texas State Parks Pass allows you and your guests unlimited access to 120 state parks and state historic sites. If you'll be doing much hiking in state parks, the pass is a real bargain compared to paying daily entrance fees. Passes are sold at most parks and historic sites, or by calling 512-389-8900. For more information, visit *www.tpwd.state .tx.us/spdest/parkinfo/passes/parkpass*. Purchasing an annual pass helps support maintenance and conservation in the state parks; in addition, many state parks have donation boxes in their offices, which allow you to support the upkeep and maintenance of that particular park. Consider contributing to the places where your favorite trails are located.

The Lower Colorado River Authority (LCRA) also offers an annual vehicle permit good for all recreation areas, including Muleshoe Bend, Grelle, and South Shore. Another option is a passbook with coupons good toward daily admission at any LCRA facility. Annual vehicle permits for parks operated by Travis County are also available.

Texas State Parks

Parks also have rules and regulations to protect each park's natural resources, as well as its visitors, including you and your dog. It is your responsibility to know the rules and regulations that apply to your use of a park. Some basics concerning pets are included here, along with sources for finding more information. On-site park staff are knowledge-able about rules and regulations, and eager to answer your questions or provide other assistance.

Texas State Parks require that dogs be on a leash not exceeding 6 feet and attended (leash in your hand) at all times. This is for the safety of wildlife, and your dog—many denizens of the parks bite back! Fines for violating the leash rule can be up to $500, which would buy

The old refectory at Palmetto State Park is one of hundreds of structures built by the Civilian Conservation Corps in state parks in the 1930s.

a lot of kibble. Rules prohibit animals from creating a disturbance or hazard within the parks. Animals are not allowed in public buildings or enclosures such as restrooms, park stores, and cabins, and dogs are not permitted in designated swimming areas or on the land or beach adjacent to the water of designated swimming areas. Dogs must have a current rabies vaccination. For details, see *www.tpwd.state.tx.us/spdest/parkinfo /rules_and_regulations.*

Lower Colorado River Authority

The Lower Colorado River Authority (LCRA), which was created by the Texas Legislature in 1934 to provide energy, water, and community services that improve the quality of life for the people of Texas, owns forty public parks and recreation areas along the Highland Lakes and Colorado River. Activities in these parks vary but often include hiking, camping, biking, and horseback riding, as well as water-related recreation such as fishing and boating. The LCRA has regulations prohibiting littering or contaminating the land or water. Pets are required to be on leash at all times in designated camping and picnic areas and "under their owner's direct control" outside of these areas. Pets are not allowed to "constitute a nuisance" anytime or anywhere, with park staff having the authority to decide whether a dog must go back on leash. Details on parks and regulations are at *www.lcra.org.*

A hitching post on Pace Bend reminds hikers and dogs that they share the trail with horses.

County Regulations

Individual counties have rules and regulations designed to keep parks and open spaces safe and enjoyable for all users, preserve the natural resources, and leave parks in good condition for future users. Most counties require dogs to be on leash except in designated areas and do not allow dogs to be obnoxious or noisy. Dogs are not typically allowed in areas where humans swim and are prohibited from disturbing wildlife or natural resources. Check with specific counties for applicable rules and regulations.

City Ordinances

Cities generally have ordinances concerning leash use and the handling of dog waste. When a hike is within the limits of a particular city, check with the parks department or other appropriate official regarding local regulations. When in doubt, keep your dog on a leash and—all together now—always scoop the poop.

Go Lightly on the Land

It cannot be said enough: Scoop up and pack out your dog's waste; or if this is absolutely not possible, bury it at least 6 inches deep. Also, pack out all of your trash, even organic matter such as orange peels. By staying on established trails, you avoid harming delicate plant and animal life and creating new trails that can contribute to erosion and lure future hikers to follow in your naughty footsteps.

Leave No Trace, a national nonprofit organization that works to help outdoor enthusiasts like us dog-loving hikers reduce their impact on the outdoors, has developed seven principles—ethical guidelines more than actual rules—that we would all do well to follow to limit negative effects on the landscape from our use of it. These are the principles, which can be found in more detail at *www.lnt.org:*

1. Plan ahead and prepare.
2. Travel and camp on durable surfaces.
3. Dispose of waste properly.
4. Leave what you find.
5. Minimize campfire impacts.
6. Respect wildlife.
7. Be considerate of other visitors.

In addition to packing out your own trash, you can help improve the outdoors by picking up and packing out other people's trash, too. The first principle—plan ahead—includes repackaging food to minimize waste. Using light, refillable containers instead of plastic bags cuts down on your trash. You can also use refillable water bottles rather than buying new water bottles every time you hike. A whopping 15 billion plastic water bottles were sold in 2002, and 88 percent of them ended up in landfills. Invest in a couple of large refillable bottles, which are readily available at outdoor stores and many other retail outlets, and fill one for you and one for your dog when you hike. Wash bottles with hot, soapy water and rinse thoroughly between each use.

Myths and Misunderstandings About Dogs

Almost all dogs love doing just about anything with their owners, and being outdoors in general. But it is a myth that all dogs are athletic and in shape. If your dog has been a couch potato, or is very young, he or she will need to be introduced gradually to the joys of hiking. Start with walks in your neighborhood, increasing the length a little at a time until your dog can easily walk several miles at a brisk pace with no ill effects, such as sore muscles or paws. It is also a myth that large dogs will have no problem with hiking, while small dogs should stick to the sidewalk. Many small dogs are very energetic and athletic (dachshunds come to mind), and even a large dog can be a couch potato.

Veronica and her pal Max are evidence that small dogs can enjoy trails like those in Government Canyon State Park.

Owners are best able to read the personalities of their dogs. Assuming your dog has a clean bill of health (that vet checkup again), don't push it if Fido doesn't seem to enjoy hiking. After all, you wouldn't drag a disinterested human friend out hiking. Friends or relatives may have dogs you can borrow as a hiking companion instead (just be sure your little "potato" still gets adequate exercise in the form of regular walks or games of fetch). Whatever size your dog, be sure to provide proper preparation and conditioning for hiking.

It is also a myth that all people love dogs. Some people simply do not like dogs, and some are actively afraid of them. Show consideration for others by keeping your dog on leash where it is required and under your control at all times. Never allow your dog to jump on other people without their express permission, and be sensitive to the reaction of strangers to your dog and respond accordingly. If dog owners are not considerate of the anti-dog types with whom we share public spaces, the unfortunate consequence may be the banning of dogs from more places.

Gear for You and Your Dog

The Boy Scouts had it right: be prepared. Even when headed out for a relatively short hike, you need to carry some basics to make the outing enjoyable and safe for you and your dog. You also should carry basic first aid and other emergency items, just in case. Following are some items that have proven essential for safe, enjoyable hiking.

Ten Essentials for You

1. Navigation tools—map and compass (and know how to use them!), GPS
2. Sun protection—sunglasses, sunscreen, and a hat
3. Insulation—extra clothing and a rain poncho
4. Illumination—headlamp or flashlight
5. First-aid supplies
6. Fire—starter and waterproof matches
7. Repair kit and tools
8. Nutrition—extra food
9. Hydration—extra water or a method to treat water
10. Emergency shelter

Ten Essentials for Your Dog

1. **Obedience training.** Before you set foot on a trail, make sure your dog is trained and can be trusted to behave when faced with other hikers, other dogs, wildlife, and an assortment of strange scents and sights in the backcountry.
2. **Doggy backpack.** Let dogs carry their own gear and water.
3. **First-aid kit.** See sidebar for a list of recommended items.
4. **Dog food/treats.** Carry more food than your dog normally consumes since he will be burning more calories than normal, and if you end up having to spend an extra night out, you need to keep the pup fed, too. Trail treats serve the same purpose for the dog as for you—quick energy and a pick-me-up during a strenuous hike.
5. **Water and water bowl.** Don't count on water along the trail for your dog. Pack enough to meet the dog's needs, too.
6. **Leash and collar or harness.** Even if your dog is absolutely trained to voice command and stays at heel without a leash, leashes are usually required by law or just common courtesy or for the safety of your dog. Have one handy at all times.

7. **Insect repellent.** One made for humans and one made for dogs, or a product that is safe for both of you.

8. **ID tags and photograph.** Your dog should always wear identification, and microchips are a great idea, as well. A vet injects a tiny encoded microchip under the skin, and if your dog ever gets lost and is picked up by animal control or taken to a vet's office, a quick pass with a scanner will reveal the chip and allow the staff to identify the dog and notify you. (Note that the process requires registration of the chip and notification if you move.) Microchips are so prevalent now that many vets and animal shelters automatically scan every unknown dog to check for chips. The photo of your dog goes in your pack and can be used to show to authorities and to make flyers to post if the dog is lost.

9. **Dog booties.** These can be used to protect your dog's feet from rough ground or harsh vegetation. They are also good for keeping bandages in place if your dog damages its pads.

10. **Compact roll of plastic bags and trowel.** Use the bags to clean up after your dog. When conditions warrant, you can use the trowel to take care of dog waste. Just pretend you are a cat—dig a hole several inches deep (well off the trail), deposit the waste, and fill in the hole.

Keeper carries her own gear on a long hike at South Llano River.

Doggy First-Aid Kit

You need a first-aid kit for your dog, even if it is just the bare essentials, for even a short nature hike. Anyone heading out into the wilderness with a canine companion, though, should carry a comprehensive canine first-aid kit with the following recommended items:

Instruments

- Scissors/bandage scissors/toenail clippers
- Rectal thermometer (a healthy rectal temp for dogs is 101°F)

Cleansers and disinfectants

- 3 percent hydrogen peroxide
- Betadine
- Canine eyewash (available at pet supply stores)

Topical antibiotics and ointments (nonprescription)

- Calamine lotion
- Triple antibiotic lotion (neomycin, bacitracin, and polymyxin)
- Baking soda (for bee stings)
- Petroleum jelly
- Stop-bleeding powder

Medications

- Enteric-coated aspirin or Bufferin
- Imodium-AD
- Pepto-Bismol

Dressings and bandages

- 4-inch gauze pads or gauze roll
- Nonstick pads
- Adhesive tape (1- and 2-inch rolls)

Miscellaneous

- Muzzle
- Dog booties
- Any prescription medications

For extended trips

Consult your veterinarian about prescription medications that may be needed in emergency situations, including oral antibiotics, eye/ear medications, emetics (to induce vomiting), pain relievers and anti-inflammatory medications, and suturing materials. Superglue can serve as emergency closing for a cleaned-out wound on a dog's pad, and vet wrap can be used to cover that up, as well as to protect sore feet on long hikes. A dog bootie can keep a dog with an injured paw walking on his or her own four feet, too, which can be a lifesaver when you are otherwise facing carrying a large dog for miles.

This footbridge over an inlet of Lake Texana is one of many water crossings Texas hikers encounter.

Food and Water

Of course, on any hike, always be prepared with water and food for your hiking partner. For really long hikes, high-energy snacks for Fido are a good idea. There are special doggy endurance bars, but banana chips without added sugar or a handful of the usual kibble work just as well and cost less. Even bits of fresh fruits such as apples or bananas are good dog snacks (but don't overdo it or you could give him diarrhea). Note that chocolate, while a great pick-me-up for human hikers, can make dogs sick and even can be lethal.

Many hikes are near creeks, rivers, lakes, or ponds that are potential sources of drinking water for your dog. Untreated water can pose health problems, however, even for dogs, from giardia, blue-green algae, and the bacteria that cause leptospirosis. The safest approach is to always carry sufficient drinking water or a method for treating water for you and your dog. It's also advisable to call veterinarians in the area where you will be hiking and ask if they have seen any of these problems recently.

Giardia is a parasite that lives in water, even very clear water, and can cause severe diarrhea. Blue-green algae are also toxic; do not let your dog drink from any body of water that has bright, blue-green (not simply green) algae present. Leptospirosis is a bacterial disease that affects people and animals, including dogs, and can be fatal. Transmitted by rodents, it is most commonly contracted through water contaminated with the urine of infected animals—by drinking it or swimming or wading in it. If local vets report outbreaks of lepto in an area, it is best to reschedule a hike for another date if you can't avoid water along the way.

Camp Care: Cleanup

Most parks in Texas provide trash cans and trash pickup, making it easy for you to leave a clean camp. If you are camping in primitive campgrounds, it will be necessary to pack out all of your trash. This includes organic matter such as fruit peels, which can attract wildlife to areas frequented by humans. Planning ahead to minimize the amount of trash you generate will make camp cleanup easier. Use refillable bottles for water and reusable containers for food—remove the packaging at home. Leave an area better than you found it by picking up any trash you see, even if it isn't yours.

Where ground fires are allowed, be sure that your campfire is completely out and cold before leaving the area. Most places do not allow the gathering of firewood, not even down and dead branches, so plan accordingly. In places that do allow you to gather firewood, be sure to take only what is already down and never break off branches or twigs, even those that appear dead.

Safety

The natural world, with its beauty and unpredictability, has the power to awe and amaze us. But it also has the power to harm us, if we are careless. Becoming lost and encountering unexpected weather have been the cause of many a ruined hike, but they don't have to be.

Routefinding

When you hike mostly in developed parks and on marked trails, it is easy to forget about the very real hazard of becoming lost. But the reality is it can happen anywhere. As a hiker, you should develop the habit of paying attention to your surroundings at all times. While on the trail, look for significant landmarks to remember, occasionally looking back to notice landmarks that will help orient you if you are retracing your steps. Looking back is especially important at trail forks. Always stay on official trails, and if you suspect you have taken a wrong turn, go back to a point where you are sure about the trail. If you do become lost, wilderness experts recommend that you find a comfortable place and wait for help to come, rather than forging on with no idea where you are going: That just makes you a moving target for rescuers. Instead, find an open place to start a signal fire (the Ten Essentials you carry with you should include fire starter). Keep track of time; after seventy-two hours of waiting, trying to find your own way out becomes the best option. That's when you'll need the map and compass that you also brought along.

Weather

There's an old saying in Texas: "If you don't like the weather, just wait a few minutes and it'll change." Dramatic and sudden changes in temperature can occur, especially in fall and spring. Thunderstorms can appear quickly in a previously clear sky, and tornadoes, hail, and strong winds can strike unexpectedly. A hike in Texas should always start with a check of the weather reports. Up-to-date reports for specific areas are available from the National Weather Service at *www.srh.noaa.gov* and *www.weather.gov.* Click on the maps to get a graphic forecast for the specific area to which you are headed. When possible, touch base with on-site staff for eyewitness reports.

Flash Floods

In the Hill Country, thunderstorms often lead to flash floods that can be deadly if you are on low ground or in washes that become filled with rushing water. In fact, flash floods are the number-one weather-related killer, accounting for some 146 deaths in the United States annually. If you are hiking and it starts raining, or you hear rushing water, move to high ground immediately.

Lightning

Lightning is another potentially deadly hazard of thunderstorms. According to the National Weather Service, lightning kills up to one hundred people each year, more than tornadoes or hurricanes. Your best bet is to know the weather forecast and reschedule your hike if there is a chance of thunderstorms, or restrict your hiking to earlier in the day since most thunderstorms form in the afternoon. If you are caught by surprise, know the conditions that can create lightning and what to do when you see it. Lightning can strike as far as 10 miles from the rain area in a thunderstorm, which is about the distance at which you can hear thunder.

If you hear thunder, seek shelter either in a hard-topped vehicle with all windows closed (do not touch any metal parts) or in a building that is completely enclosed, with a roof, walls, and floor. Stay away from anything connected to the plumbing or electrical wiring of the building, as the wiring and plumbing can carry current from a strike into the ground. Wait at least thirty minutes after the last thunderclap before leaving shelter. Do not seek shelter under partly enclosed structures such as tents or picnic shelters, and do not seek shelter under tall, isolated trees. In fact, stay away from all tall, isolated objects, as that is what lightning usually strikes (including you standing in an open field). Also stay away from metal objects such as fence posts, trail markers, and metal-frame backpacks, as metal is an excellent conductor (remove jewelry). In addition to the visible flash, current travels along the ground and this is what strikes many victims. If you are caught in the open, get in the "desperation position": Crouch down with feet together and knees bent, bend your head down to touch your knees, and put your hands over the back of your head. With you in this position, your dog is probably lower than you are, or at least about the same height. Hold on tight to his leash and try to keep him on all fours, not sitting or lying down. Do not lie on the ground yourself, either.

Tornadoes

Tornadoes are another dangerous weather phenomenon that Texas hikers could encounter. Again, check weather forecasts before heading out. If thunderstorms develop, watch for an obvious funnel cloud. Sometimes tornadoes have no funnel, so watch for strong, persistent rotation in the cloud base; whirling dust or debris on the ground; hail or heavy rain followed by dead calm or a swift wind shift; or a loud rumble that doesn't fade in a few seconds like thunder does. If you detect any of these, seek shelter in a sturdy building, if possible, positioning yourself at the bottom and center of the structure, crouched on the ground with your head covered. If there is no shelter available, lie flat and facedown on low ground with your arms over the back of your head. Get as far away from trees as you can, as they can be blown about by a tornado. Vehicles are extremely dangerous in a tornado; do not seek shelter in a vehicle and get as far away from it as you can. Do not seek shelter under bridges; winds can be more severe under a bridge due to the constricted airflow.

Hurricanes

On the Gulf Coast, hurricane season officially runs from June 1 through November 30. During this time of year, never head out on a hike along the coast without checking whether tropical storms or hurricanes are forecast to reach the area in the next day or two. If an area has been hit by a hurricane recently, call ahead and check on conditions. Not only can trails flood out or be blocked by debris left behind by storm surges, but hurricane winds break trees and limbs and leave damaged trees that are in imminent danger of falling—poetically called "widow makers" by foresters. Storms can also relocate wildlife, meaning you could encounter an alligator or confused snake in an unexpected place. Heed the warnings of land managers and reschedule a hike if the area has suffered hurricane damage and may not be safe.

Heat

Temperatures in many parts of Texas can exceed 100°F in summer months, which, combined with high humidity levels and a blazing sun, can be a recipe for disaster. Humans and dogs need to drink plenty of water in the heat. Avoid hiking in midday, rest in the shade, and don't overdo it. Use plenty of sunscreen to avoid a painful souvenir of your hike.

The cool, clear waters of Can Creek in Lost Maples State Natural Area keep Max from overheating.

Many Hill Country trails are rugged and scenic.

Using This Book

This guidebook gives you an overview of each hike, what you can expect to see, and a little bit about what the experience will be like.

For each hike, the distance given is for a loop route or a round-trip, out-and-back hike, unless otherwise noted. The hiking time is intended as a guideline and is based on a pace of about 2 miles per hour, with stops factored in to enjoy a view and for lunch and water breaks on longer hikes. Many of us hike at a faster pace, and the times given are generally conservative, meaning you should safely be able to complete the hike in that amount of time or less.

Elevation ranges are given so you will have an idea of how much effort you can expect to expend on the hike. The difficulty rating takes into account how rugged the trail is (uneven and rocky versus smooth dirt, for example), how hilly the route is, and to some extent, the length of the hike. Your own assessment of the difficulty will depend on your physical fitness and that of your dog. The more you hike, the easier the trails will seem.

Dagger Point Trail offers a view of San Antonio Bay at the Aransas National Wildlife Refuge.

Hikes rated easy are mostly flat terrain and level surfaces; moderate trails have some uphill stretches or an uneven, rugged surface; and difficult hikes involve significant elevation change, rugged surfaces, or longer distances, or all three.

Relevant rules and regulations are noted. Each write-up mentions the trail surface you'll be hiking on, so you'll know whether your dog's paws are up to it, how much shade you can expect, and whether and where you'll encounter water.

You'll need a more detailed map than what is presented in this book, as these maps are intended to give you only a general idea of the route and landmarks. In most cases, good trail maps are available at the property, and the availability of trail maps is noted in this book as well.

Canine health information came from Lori Haug, of the Texas A&M University School of Veterinary Medicine and Biomedical Sciences, The Humaner Trainer in Austin, and basic dog-care books, including *The Little Guides: Dogs,* edited by Paul McGreevy. The Texas Parks and Wildlife Department provided information on snakes, alligators, and other wildlife. The National Weather Service Houston/Galveston office assisted with weather information and safety guidelines.

How the Trails Were Selected

The hikes in this book are all convenient to Austin, San Antonio, or Houston and are, for the most part, well marked and easy to follow or located in places where it would be hard to get truly lost. These hikes offer a variety of lengths, level of challenge, terrain, and interesting sights to see. Most provide an opportunity to see wildlife, stunning views, unusual sights, or beautiful landscapes.

Enjoy the Trails: Get Involved

Most of Texas land is in private hands. The state is blessed, though, with a wonderful network of state parks, county parks, and other areas that are accessible to the public for recreation such as hiking. The continued availability of much of this land depends on the vocal support of the public, however. Let your elected officials know that you visit and enjoy public parks. Pay entrance fees, even when there is only an "iron ranger" on duty. Ask park rangers what you can do to help them and their parks—whether that means showing up for a workday or writing a letter in support of more funding for the park. Dig the change out of your pocket and drop it in the donation boxes located at all state parks; you'll be helping the park and lightening your load at the same time.

Almost all state parks have opportunities for volunteers, including park hosts, tour guides, office assistance, and trail maintenance, for which training is provided. For more information, contact the park manager or volunteer coordinator at the park of your choice. Many Texas state parks also have nonprofit friends groups or other support organizations. Find out more about these at *www.tpwd.state.tx.us/spdest/friends_groups*.

Some trails are maintained and upgraded by volunteer organizations such as the Memorial Park Conservancy (Houston) and Friends of Bull Creek (Austin). If you enjoy one of these trails, please support these organizations with a donation or by volunteering for a trail cleanup workday (check websites).

A Note About Safety

Safety is an important concern in all outdoor activities. No guidebook can alert you to every hazard or anticipate the limitations of every reader. Therefore, the descriptions of roads, trails, routes, and natural features in this book are not representations that a particular place or excursion will be safe for your party. When you follow any of the routes described in this book, you assume responsibility for your own safety. Under normal conditions, such excursions require the usual attention to traffic, road and trail conditions, weather, terrain, the capabilities of your party, and other factors. Keeping informed on current conditions and exercising common sense are the keys to a safe, enjoyable outing.

The Mountaineers Books

PART 2

The Trails

AUSTIN

1. Emma Long Metropolitan Park, Turkey Creek Trail

Distance: 2.9 miles round trip
Hiking time: 1.5 hours
Difficulty: Easy to moderate
High point: 650 feet
Elevation gain: 250 feet
Best hiking season: Year-round
Regulations: Dogs are allowed off leash but must be under owner's control
Map: USGS Austin West 7.5' Quadrangle
Contact: Emma Long Metropolitan Park, 512-346-1831, *www.ci.austin.tx.us/parks*

Getting there: From downtown Austin, take Loop 1 (MoPac) north to the Ranch Road 2222 exit. Head west on RR 2222 for 4 miles, just past Loop 360, and turn left at City Park Road. Follow this winding road roughly 4 miles to a park sign on the right, then about a half mile farther to the parking area for the trailhead, marked Turkey Creek Nature Trail.

Notes: Emma Long Metropolitan Park, on the shore of Lake Austin, has camping, picnic areas, two boat ramps, a fishing pier, swimming beach, restrooms, and showers. There are restrooms and water fountains in the main park (the entrance booth is another half mile down the road from the trailhead), which has an entrance fee, and dogs must be on leash. There is no entrance fee at the trailhead, but there are no services, either.

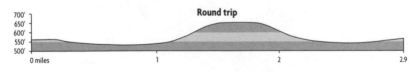

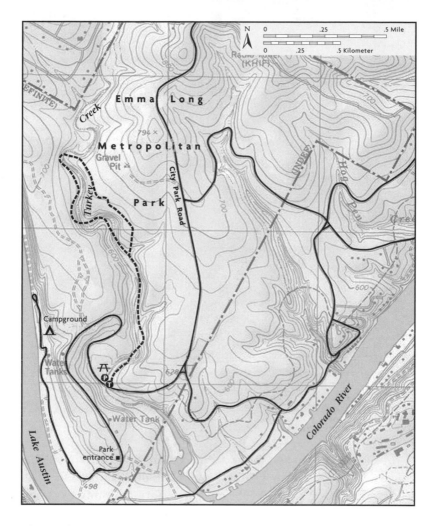

This trail is just minutes from the heart of the city, but once you leave the parking area, that is easy to forget. The only sounds you and your dog will hear are the gurgling of Turkey Creek, the breeze through the trees, and birdsong—along with the occasional splashing of a pup who cannot resist a quick swim in the clear water, which flows year-round. The route follows the shallow, meandering creek and crosses it multiple times, and this is a leash-free area, so your dog is free to wade and swim to his heart's content. Rocks and human-made stepping-stones make it possible for you to cross with dry feet, unless it has rained a lot lately. (Avoid the trail in times of heavy rain; call ahead to check conditions.)

Max cools his paws crossing Turkey Creek.

The trail is wooded and the surface mostly soft dirt with occasional rocky scrambles. A shady picnic area just a short distance from the trailhead and a wooden bench about a mile along are nice resting spots, and there are plenty of rocks perfect for sitting on while your dog swims or explores. The trail forks at about three-quarters of a mile; stay to the left. Just past the 1-mile marker, the hike leaves the stream and heads uphill a bit to a more open area with cedar breaks and occasional views.

In spring and fall, enjoy the wildflowers, but watch for cactus. When the trail descends the bluff back to the stream, log-reinforced steps make it easy going for two- and four-legged hikers. The loop reconnects to the original trail just before a 2.3-mile marker, where you head back out the way you came in. You are likely to meet other dogs in the parking lot, so have your leash handy, and pat yourself on the back for putting that towel in the car to dry your pup with before heading home.

2. Barton Creek Greenbelt

Distance: 7.25 miles one way
Hiking time: 4 hours
Difficulty: Moderate
High point: 830 feet
Elevation gain: 340 feet
Best hiking season: Year-round
Regulations: Dogs must be on leash
Map: Austin Parks and Recreation, Barton Creek Greenbelt
Contact: City of Austin Parks and Recreation Department,
512-974-6700, *www.ci.austin.tx.us/parks*

Getting there: The Barton Springs trailhead is at the far end of the Barton Springs Pool parking lot in Zilker Park, 2100 Barton Springs Road, in Austin.

Notes: Do not leave valuables in your car at trailheads. Access points to the greenbelt are at Barton Springs Pool, Spyglass Road, Loop 360, Gaines/Twin Falls, and Trails End. Restrooms and water are at Barton Springs and Spyglass, and restrooms are near Trails End. The creek is subject to flooding; call ahead to check conditions.

This greenbelt, smack in the middle of an urban area, is surprisingly wild and quiet. About the only sound along much of the route will be birds, a lot of them. The entire trail, from one end to the other, is 7.25 miles, but there are four access points, allowing hikers the chance to vary the distance. Maps of the trail are posted at most trailheads, and mile markers have been placed at quarter-mile intervals on the trail, although some have been washed away or obscured by vegetation. Hike out and back, or arrange for transportation at another point along the way for a shorter distance.

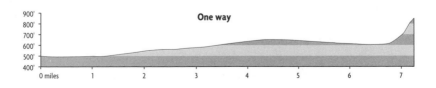

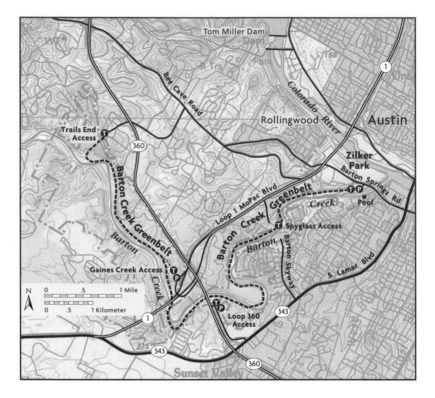

From the Barton Springs parking lot, the trail heads up Barton Creek, which is dry here much of the year, quickly heading into the shade of tall trees. Hard-core runners, other dogs and their humans, and mountain bikers are usually out in force, especially in nice weather. Soon, there are cliffs on your right, with some development visible on the top, then a bench, which is a good place to rest, overlooking what is a nice swimming hole when there has been enough rain. Numerous splits lead from the trail down to the creek, but stay on the main trail, which is generally wider, or you and your dog will have to scramble over a lot of rocks. The vegetation opens up and the trail becomes very rocky, then you cross the creek, which, again, is more often dry than not. Then you encounter the first of many splits between foot and bike routes; the foot routes have rough cedar rails narrowing access and are generally best for you and your dog, as you won't have to watch for fast-moving cyclists. You cross the creek again and head back into the trees, with a high cliff on the right. Stay close to the creekbed unless you want to rock climb, which you are likely to see people doing in a serious manner.

The hike and bike parts rejoin, then pass through a heavily wooded area. There is access to the Spyglass trailhead here, about 1 mile from Barton Springs. Then hike into cedar woods more typical of the area, through another hike–bike split and then some heavy brush along a bluff above the creek. At 2.75 miles, there is a very wide, rocky creek crossing, then the trail goes over a side creek, which will have water after rains, on a wooden bridge. More cliffs rise on the right, and the trail goes under—way under—Loop 360 (another access point, about 3 miles from Barton Springs) and becomes narrow and winding. Enjoy the butterflies and dragonflies, then the interesting cliffs on your left with overhangs, collapses, and clinging ferns. On one stretch of about 10 yards, a chain is fastened to the cliff as a handhold to help you maneuver the narrow trail. Hold on tight to your dog.

The trail then goes under another highway, Loop 1 or MoPac; the bridge was designed to limit disturbance to the greenbelt. Even in dry times, there is a pool of water here for doggie refreshment, and this is usually an easy place to cross. Or continue along for another quarter mile

Hikers on the upper Barton Creek Greenbelt can enjoy still pools and waterfalls year-round.

to Twin Falls and cross the creek. To end your hike here, turn right on the other side and follow the path along the creek, then up a rugged, rocky path uphill to the Gaines Creek trailhead and parking area. You have hiked about 4 miles. Otherwise, after crossing at Twin Falls, turn left to continue heading upstream. The trail is hard-packed dirt with some rocky patches, and many user-created routes branching down to the creek. In general, follow the wider, higher route. A high cliff rises on your right, often close to the trail, and the heavily wooded area has some impressive oaks. About a half mile farther, you reach a stretch where there is water in the creek most of the time, thanks to springs, with several waterfalls and still pools reflecting the sky. Floods have created strangely twisted and bent trees along the creek. Just before the intersection with Trails End access is a turnoff to primitive restrooms; then, if you are finishing at Trails End, it is almost a half-mile scramble up a steep, rocky slope to the trailhead. Or, continue about a half mile along the creek to the trail's end, marked by a nice waterfall, then turn and retrace your steps to wherever you have arranged to end your hike.

3. Bull Creek Greenbelt Trail

Distance: 3 miles one way
Hiking time: 1.5 hours
Difficulty: Easy
High point: 625 feet
Elevation gain: 30 feet
Best hiking season: Year-round
Regulations: Dogs must be on leash
Map: Austin Parks and Recreation, Lower Bull Creek Greenbelt and
   District Park
Contact: City of Austin Parks and Recreation Department,
   512-974-6700; *www.bullcreek.net*

Getting there: From Loop 360, between US Highway 183 and Ranch Road 2222, take Spicewood Springs Road east (a right turn if you're headed north on Loop 360, left if headed south), then take the next right onto Old Spicewood Springs Road. You'll pass an apartment complex on the left, then the trailhead. Just past that, turn into the parking lot on your right.

Notes: Do not leave valuables in your car.

One way

700'
650'
600'
550'
500'

0 miles   1   2   3

A short, level stretch of trail, with rough post fencing on either side closing off areas under restoration, takes you to steps down to a narrow crossing, the first of several, this one over Stillhouse Creek, a spring-fed stream that flows year-round. The packed-dirt and rock trail heads up two sets of steps, past a fork to the right that leads to the water, then levels out, and you and your dog have a nice walk ahead. You will emerge from the trees and walk through expanses of wildflowers (most of the year) and a couple more wooded stretches, over some cedar post bridges, and then come to Bull Creek, which you will be more or less following the rest of the way. There is a wide, shallow water crossing under the trees and, inexplicably, a red fire hydrant smack in the middle of it. If your pup wants to take a minute to check out this oddity, feel free to let him. By stepping on stones, you can keep your feet dry on this crossing most of the time.

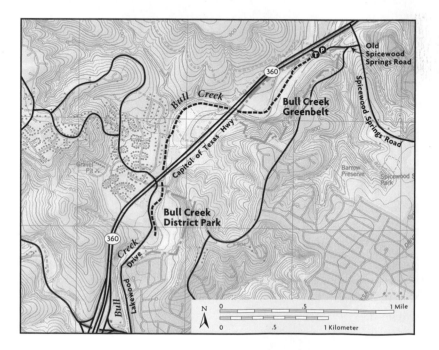

The next section is dirt trail hemmed in closely by thick brush. A beautiful high cliff rises on your left at one point, until you reach another creek crossing, off to the left before the overpass, where you are likely to

Stillhouse Creek is the first of several crossings on a hike in the Bull Creek Greenbelt.

get your feet wet. Loop 360 passes overhead here, and although the traffic noise may be disconcerting to some dogs, the swallows nesting under the overpass are worth a few minutes of observation. Take advantage of the smooth rock surface and open area before passing under the bridge to spend some time doing this, and to dry your feet from the creek crossing. Then look for the trail marker—the trail heads up slightly from the creek—and continue.

A short distance farther, you will cross a road; there are restrooms and an information kiosk here, as well as parking and access from Loop 360. The trail narrows here and hugs the creek for a ways. Part of it is smooth stone, but it is mostly dirt, which can become mud from spring seeps or if there has been any rain. There are numerous access points to the water if your dog likes to swim and you want to hang out, but some of the trail passes through the Balcones Canyonlands Preserve, so it is best to restrict your hiking to the main trail.

You will soon leave behind the traffic noise and can hear many birds. Shade alternates with open areas, and you will pass a fork where a trail goes right and stepping blocks cross over the creek. This way leads to a hiking trail through the preserve, which is closed to dogs, so continue without crossing the creek, following markers for the hiking trail. Apartments and an office building appear on your left, mostly behind trees, then you will see another Loop 360 overpass ahead. Just before you reach it, there is another fork, with markers indicating that a bike trail continues straight, while the hiking trail turns right to cross the creek. Once you cross, turn left and walk under the double overpass into a parking area. This is another Loop 360 access point, and this part of the creek has nice waterfalls and swimming holes. Enjoy these, and when you are ready to continue, avoid what seem to be trails close to the creek; these are generally quite muddy and not the official route. Instead, walk toward the road from the creek to find a trail marker. A couple of stretches pass through tall trees and about 100 yards along Lakewood Drive, then you head into Bull Creek District Park. The park has picnic tables, restrooms, and plenty of grassy area for dogs to run and frolic—this is an off-leash park from the area behind the restrooms all the way to the creek.

An old concrete dam across the creek near the parking lot is a nice place to slip off your boots and soak your feet in the cool water. From here, retrace your steps back to where you started, unless you planned ahead and have a car waiting at this end.

4. Southeast Metropolitan Park, Primitive Trail

Distance: 2.2-mile loop
Hiking time: 1.5 hours
Difficulty: Easy to moderate
High point: 537 feet
Elevation gain: 110 feet
Best hiking season: Year-round
Regulations: Dogs must be on leash; scoop and pack out waste
Map: USGS Webberville 7.5' Quadrangle
Contact: Travis County Parks, 512-854-9383,
   www.co.travis.tx.us/tnr/parks/southeast_metro.asp

Getting there: Take State Highway 71 east from Austin, past the airport and through Del Valle. Drive about 1.5 miles past the intersection with Farm to Market Road 973 and the entrance to the park is on your left. Turn right just past the park entrance and follow the road around the ball fields to the trailhead parking area.

Notes: No services at the trailhead, but there are restrooms near the soccer fields (to the left just after you enter the park). Hours change seasonally, so call ahead for current hours.

This hike offers a variety of sights and sounds, and with numbered markers every 200 feet, you will always know just how far you and your pooch have traveled and how much hike you have left. From the parking lot, follow the wide, crushed-granite trail past trees and cactus to a shaded overlook. The view is far and, if you look west, the Capitol and University of Texas tower are visible. The trail starts just before the overlook, with stone steps leading down to the right. A short stretch of narrow dirt trail Ts into the loop. Turn left to follow the numbered markers in order (or right if you are the rebellious type).

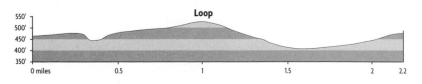

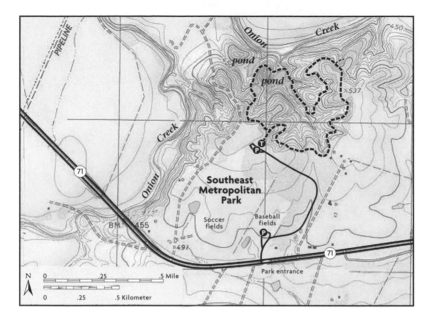

The trail heads down and crosses the first of a number of wooden bridges. There are also many benches, both typical park style and others that are rustic logs on supports. The trail follows gently rolling hills, with a lot of up and down, passing through both wooded and open areas. Head up from the bridge into a wooded stretch where you can listen to the creak of cedar trees in the breeze and look for web traps on the ground. Just before marker 13 is a pond ringed with cattails where you might startle a large frog on the shore. Catch-and-release fishing is allowed on this and another pond on the route, and wooden platforms are provided. These also make nice spots from which to observe the ponds, as the shore is marshy and often muddy (which means there is no easy access for your dog to drink, so plan on carrying water for him). The trail follows a gravel road to the next pond and turns left just before a covered platform over the water, and then goes along a levee before crossing a spillway to pass another overlook and bench. You then cross a gully full of large rocks and trace a hillside through open areas of cactus and grasses, with wooded hills on every side blocking all signs of the nearby city. This stretch is mostly wooded, and you might catch a glimpse of a white cottontail, or the flash of a cardinal. Just past marker 35 is a turnoff to a group camping area (reservations required; contact the parks department). Near marker 38, the trail emerges from the trees and a bench and platform make it

Two tranquil ponds ringed with cattails reward hikers on Southeast Metropolitan Park's Primitive Trail.

easy to enjoy a nice view of downtown Austin from this high point.

After another stretch through the trees, steps lead down a steep hillside to a drainage, and then back up; the steps are large and very small dogs may need help here. As the trail rises and falls and goes into the trees and back out, you cross other gullies and enjoy views of the surrounding hills (the "view" at marker 47, though, is of a cement plant). There are more twists and turns on this side of the loop as the trail goes up and down and crosses bridges. Small animals rustling in the brush, fallen trees, and scents left behind by wildlife give your dog plenty of interesting things to sniff. The trail is mostly dirt with some areas of grass and some of rocks, with the occasional chunk of flint.

Just after marker 62, you are back at the T intersection with the trail from the parking lot. Just before you get to the lot, another trail to the right leads to a wildlife blind down by another pond. It is 0.3 mile each way to the blind.

5. Richard Moya Park

Distance: 2-mile loop
Hiking time: 45 minutes
Difficulty: Easy
High point: 500 feet
Elevation gain: 10 feet
Best hiking season: Year-round
Regulations: Dogs must be on leash
Map: USGS Montopolis 7.5' Quadrangle
Contact: Travis County Parks, 512-854-9383,
  www.co.travis.tx.us/tnr/parks/richard_moya.asp

Getting there: From the intersection of State Highway 71 and US Highway 183 near the Austin airport, take US 183 south 2.6 miles and turn left onto Burleson Road. It is 1.2 miles to the park entrance on the right, easily recognized by a blinking yellow caution light and General Aviation Boulevard on the left.

Notes: Avoid contact with creek water, which can contain hazardous materials from runoff.

Turn left after entering and find a shady spot to park. Just twenty minutes from downtown Austin, these 100 acres of blackland prairie are covered in hundreds of majestic pecan trees and bordered by Onion Creek. Although the trail is paved, the grassy, wooded setting makes for a very pleasant hike, one that is ideal for young pups, owners new to the hiking crowd, or those who haven't been out in a while. It is also a good spot to get in a quick hike and maybe a picnic in scenic surroundings when you don't have time to go farther. Start from near the restrooms closest to the entrance and head clockwise on the walkway under towering trees to a playground and group picnic area. This area is likely to be full of people on nice weekends, so hold on to the leash.

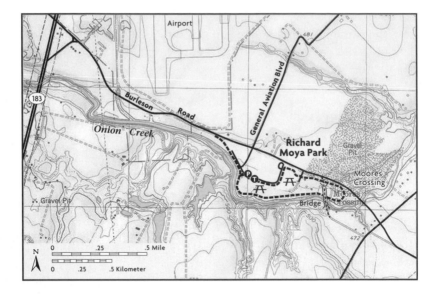

Just on the other side of this busy area is Moore's Crossing Bridge, worth a quick detour. The metal spans holding up the bridge were originally part of a bridge built across the Colorado River at Congress Avenue in 1884. That bridge was dismantled in 1910 and the spans put in storage. Three of them were installed here over Onion Creek in 1915, only to be destroyed by flood that same year; the spans you see now were placed in 1922. Walk onto the bridge for a nice view of the creek and surrounding park, and a lot of interesting smells for your dog. Then double back and continue on down the trail, passing under the bridge and through more pecan trees. In fall, there likely will be people collecting pecans all over the park. Gathering the nuts from the ground is allowed, but disturbing the trees is not. Some dogs love pecans; take two and squeeze them in your hand to crack the shells and see if yours is one of them. Just be sure to take and consume in moderation.

The trail loops around and passes back under the bridge, then follows the creek through more trees, past picnic tables and grills. There will be several places to access the water, but it is deep and generally not of a good enough quality to let your dog drink it. Mileage markers every quarter mile help you track your progress back to where you started. A spur trail leads past a couple of lighted ball fields (these are closed on Fridays and from December 15 to February 15, something to keep in mind when scheduling your hike) to a heavily wooded picnic area, a good place to wander in the

The metal spans of Moore's Crossing Bridge, over Onion Creek in Richard Moya Park, were originally part of a bridge on Congress Avenue in the 1800s.

soft grass, listen to and watch for the many birds, and enjoy the shade. The trail leads up a small hill to the edge of the park, where it connects to an asphalt bike trail that goes to McKinney Falls State Park and beyond (go to *www.ci.austin.tx.us/bicycle/bikemap.htm* and click on D-3 for details). Follow the path back to your car whenever you're ready. This park is close to the airport, so you may hear airplanes overhead, but it is not in the direct flight path, so the noise level is very tolerable.

HIGHLAND LAKES

6. Pace Bend County Park

Distance: 3.5-mile loop
Hiking time: 1.75 hours
Difficulty: Easy
High point: 800 feet
Elevation gain: 90 feet
Best hiking season: Year-round
Regulations: Dogs are allowed off leash, but must be under the owner's control; noisy, vicious, or dangerous animals are not permitted; dispose of dog waste and trash in receptacles provided
Map: USGS Pace Bend 7.5' Quadrangle
Contact: Travis County Parks, Pace Bend Park, 512-264-1482, *www.co.travis.tx.us/tnr/parks/pace_bend.asp*

Getting there: From Austin, take State Highway 71 west about 11 miles past Ranch Road 620 to Pace Bend Road (Ranch Road 2322). There is a stoplight at this intersection and signs indicating the park. Turn right and go approximately 4 miles to where the road enters the park.

Notes: The park is owned by the Lower Colorado River Authority (LCRA) and operated by Travis County. Entrance fee. The park closes to day visitors at 9:00 PM. Respect no trespassing signs on private camps adjacent to the park.

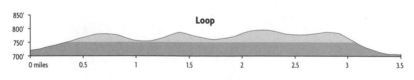

This hike explores the high ground of a 1368-acre park occupying the tip of a 4-mile-long peninsula on the western shore of Lake Travis, which is formed by Mansfield Dam on the Colorado River. The shoreline on the west side of the peninsula is high limestone cliffs, while gentle slopes and beaches are the rule on the east side. This popular park can be crowded on weekends and in the summer, but on weekdays the rest of the year, you and your dog are likely to have it mostly to yourselves. Other than at the trailheads, the trails are not clearly marked, but park staff encourage hikers to feel free to explore and the area is bounded on all sides by a circular park road, so you'll never be lost for long.

The hike takes you in a clockwise direction, with the road and lake on your left at all times, which should make it easy to get your bearings even if you do not follow the route exactly as outlined here. Sharp-eyed hikers are likely to see deer, raccoon, fox, jackrabbits, and dozens of birds. Keep your dog in sight and under control in case he happens upon one of these animals. Once inside the park, turn right at Grisham Trail (a

The trailhead at Pace Bend County Park invites hikers and dogs into the semi-wooded hills.

park road) and drive several miles to parking for a trailhead across from
Mudd Cove and Tournament Point. Just a little farther down the road,
there are restrooms at the turnoff for this day-use area, which is also a
nice place to take a dip in the lake after your hike. Study the map posted
at the trailhead, then follow the trail into the juniper breaks and up the
hill. Horseback riders also use the rock and dirt trail; in fact, the trails
frequented by horses are the most obvious and easy to follow in the park.
You will be walking through alternating open and shady stretches, and
dogs will find plenty of interesting scents along the way. At a T intersection where there is a hitching post, turn left to start your circle.

The route roughly follows a loop shown on the map. At the far end
of the loop, a wide road heads straight and down the hill, but continue
circling to the right here. As you curve around on the other side of the
hill, there are nice views through the trees. At some point, the loop on
the map veers back to the T intersection, but the more obvious horse trail

continues straight until it reaches the park road, about 30 yards from another trailhead. Stay on this route, turn right at the road, and walk to that trailhead. This circles another hill for a short distance, through a motte of tall trees and over some small rocky scrambles. Again, the map shows the hiking trail looping around to connect with the trail you first came in on, but the horse trail will take you onto the road. When you reach it this time, turn right and follow the road past the restrooms and back to your car.

If you and your pooch are in the mood for more, just head back into the trees. You can go right at the T intersection this time, or just explore along any open passages. Small pyramids of rock were used to mark the original hiking route, and some of these can still be found. You can spend some time letting your dog romp on the lakeshore in the day-use area, but remember to keep him under your control and clean up any messes. No lifeguards are on duty, so swimming is at your own risk. Drinking water is available across from the Tatum Cove boat ramp on Grisham Road—look for the shape of an old-timey well.

7. Grelle Recreation Area

Distance: 2-mile balloon loop
Hiking time: 1 hour
Difficulty: Easy
High point: 820 feet
Elevation gain: 180 feet
Best hiking season: Year-round
Regulations: Dogs must be on leash in designated camping and picnic areas; outside these areas, dogs must be under owner's control; park staff may request that a dog be put on leash; no glass
Map: USGS Spicewood 7.5' Quadrangle
Contact: Lower Colorado River Authority, 512-473-3200 or 800-776-5272, *www.lcra.org/community/grelle.html*

Getting there: Take State Highway 71 west from Austin approximately 30 miles (cross the Pedernales River/Lake Travis). Turn right onto Spur 191 to the tiny town of Spicewood, and then right onto County Road 404. Drive about a mile and turn left onto County Road 412, which dead-ends into the park.

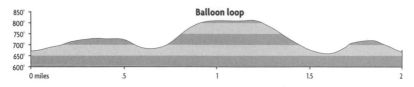

Notes: Entrance fee. Composting toilets in camping area. No drinking water available. There are picnic tables and fire rings in the park, and horseback riding is allowed, although not on the hiking trail.

This Lower Colorado River Authority (LCRA) recreation area hugs an isolated cove on the south shore of Lake Travis, with a grassy beach good for swimming and a 2-mile hiking trail to a plateau with views of the lake. At the park entrance, turn right and follow the gravel road through the campground to the trailhead, indicated by a brown fiberglass marker.

The narrow trail winds above the lake, hugging the side of the juniper-covered hills. It begins as crushed granite that quickly gives way to a rocky surface that alternates with dirt, heading up and down then leveling off to pass beneath some sizeable oaks. You will then cross a narrow inlet of the lake that is often dry, then continue on more level ground and across a rocky streambed, also usually dry. The trail turns away from the stream-bed and follows a narrow, rocky drainage. You cross this, then circle below

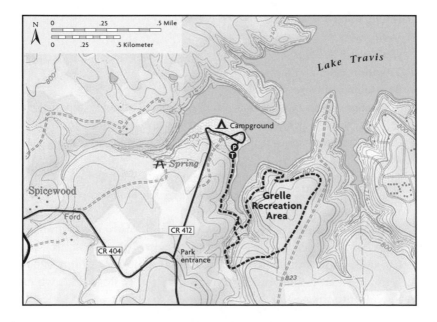

a high ledge of rocks that no doubt makes an impressive waterfall after a rain, with a deep depression at the bottom of it that remains muddy even in dry times. The trail climbs up steps on the side of the wash to flat rock at the top, crosses that, and reenters the trees, where it continues to ascend, passing some low rocky ledges. It levels off, and before long you reach a fork, where you veer left (straight ahead takes you to a dirt road that eventually leads out of the park).

This section winds through thick cedar brush on a mostly level dirt surface, where raccoon and deer tracks are often visible. You and your dog will also see plenty of evidence that cows and horses sometimes wander into the area from nearby ranches. At another fork, continue to bear left, through taller trees, winding around on a high slope above the lake, which you can glimpse through the trees, now on your right. Another fork offers the option of reconnecting with the trail on top of the hill and retracing your steps back from there. Instead, turn right and head down the slope on the cedar-log steps, threading through boulders and

A sinkhole on the trail in the Grelle Recreation Area becomes a waterfall after it rains.

down loose rock along the side of the hill. As you hike toward the end of a point, the trail appears to fork around a tree. Stay to the left (the right is just a quick way down to the water) and continue down more steps to emerge in the tall grass and scattered trees of the shore. The trail merges with a double track, crosses a dry streambed, and reconnects with the original trail to form a balloon loop. Turn right to head back to your car, about a quarter mile away.

8. Muleshoe Bend Recreation Area

Distance: 3.5-mile loop, with longer options
Hiking time: Varies
Difficulty: Moderate
High point: 740 feet
Elevation gain: 50 feet
Best hiking season: Year-round
Regulations: Dogs must be on leash in designated camping and picnic areas; outside these areas, dogs must be under owner's control; park staff may request that a dog be put on leash; no glass
Map: LCRA Muleshoe Bend Recreation Area
Contact: Lower Colorado River Authority, 512-473-3200 or 800-776-5272, *www.lcra.org/community/muleshoe_bend.html*

Getting there: Take State Highway 71 west from Austin, turn right onto Paleface Ranch Road (about 1 mile after crossing the Pedernales Bridge). Drive 4.5 miles and turn right onto County Road 414, which winds 1.5 miles, with a sharp right bend at Ridge Harbor, before it dead-ends into the park.

Notes: Entrance fee. Restrooms and drinking water, including a low faucet for dogs, at the park entrance. The campgrounds allow tent camping and have picnic tables, fire rings, and composting toilets. The gentle

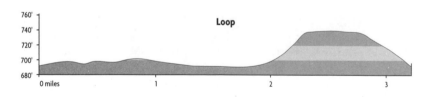

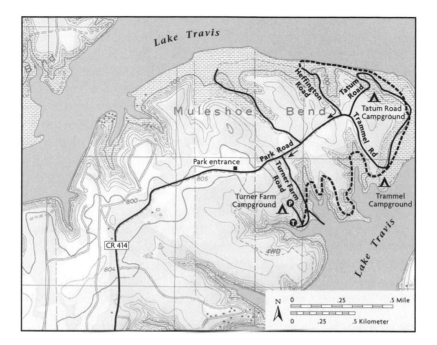

shoreline is conducive to swimming in warm weather. The peninsula is covered in gnarly oaks and junipers, grassy areas and brush, several types of cactus, and hills and rocks in an amazing variety of sizes and colors.

There is a rugged, 6.5-mile mountain bike trail in the park, but for safety reasons dogs are not allowed on that trail. Instead, you and your pup can explore the 6 miles of shoreline and any of the rest of the 900 acres on this peninsula into Lake Travis. One way to do this is to take the first right turn after the park entrance, Turner Farm Road, and follow it down to the Turner Farm Campground on the shore. Find a shady spot to park and start following the shoreline in a counterclockwise direction—with the lake on your right and the wooded hills on your left. Once you are away from these camping areas, you can let your dog run free as long as she is under your control and is not a "nuisance."

You and your dog can hike around to the other side of the peninsula as far as you like, then turn and retrace your steps, or, you can round the point and then take park roads back across the hills to make a lopsided loop. Depending on the level of the water (the Lake Travis waterline rises and falls depending on a variety of factors, including rainfall and the rate of release of water through Mansfield Dam; check lake levels at *www.lcra .org*), you will have several options for your way around the point. One is to follow the dirt and rock road that roughly traces the edge of the hills, with gentle ups and downs and some shade. Another is to keep close to the water line, walking on mostly flat and sandy shore, where you are likely to see the tracks of deer and other animals and where you can let your dog drink or cool his paws in the water. A third option is to traverse the wide, grassy slope in between (just watch for uneven ground and rocks hidden in the grass). When the lake is at normal levels or below, all three options will be available, and it is generally easy to switch back and forth between them.

From Turner Farm Campground, circumvent two deep inlets of the lake to reach Trammel Campground. After this, you and your dog will be making a wide, long semicircle along the edge of the peninsula, which is formed by a large bend in Lake Travis that is named, of course, Muleshoe Bend. As you round the point and pass the Tatum Road Campground, decide between the shore and a dirt road near the hillside, as the in-be-

Raccoons leave clear tracks in the soft dirt found on some parts of the trail at Muleshoe Bend Recreation Area.

tween grassy area is often covered in chest-high vegetation. If you follow the sandy shore, you will likely see more animal tracks and encounter a variety of birds. A short way along the other side of the peninsula, there will be a dirt double track heading to the left, back toward the hill. Follow it back to the dirt road and turn right, pass one little valley, then turn in at the next one, which is Heffington Road. This rocky road heads uphill, where the bike trail crosses it, then continues to the main park road. Just to the left is Trammel Road, which leads to the shore and the campground you walked through earlier. Turn right to take the park road back to Turner Farm Road and follow it back to where you parked.

9. Arkansas Bend Park

Distance: 2–4 miles round trip
Hiking time: Up to 2 hours
Difficulty: Easy
High point: 700 feet
Elevation gain: 50 feet (depends on lake level)
Best hiking season: Year-round
Regulations: Dogs must be on leash
Map: USGS Mansfield Dam 7.5′ Quadrangle
Contact: Travis County Parks, 512-854-PARK,
www.co.travis.tx.us/tnr/parks/arkansas_bend.asp

Getting there: From Austin, take US Highway 183 north to Cedar Park and then follow Farm to Market Road 1431 south 11 miles to Lohmans Ford Road in Lago Vista. Turn left and drive about 5 miles to Sylvester Ford Road. Turn left again and drive 1.5 miles to the park.

Notes: Entrance fee; fee booth open during peak season (summer) and on weekends. Chemical toilets, no drinking water. Primitive camping; reservations not required. The water level in Lake Travis varies according to rainfall and dam releases. Check lake level at *www.lcra.org*. This hike is best when the level is at or below 681 feet.

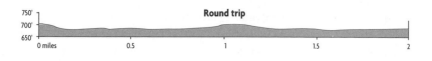

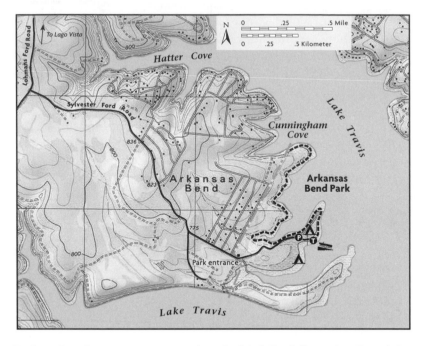

Rather than being a more typical trail, this hike follows 2 miles of the lakeshore in this 323-acre park on upper Lake Travis, and depending on the lake level, you and your dog will be walking on a mixture of rock, sand, and grass. Start from the boat ramp parking area (watch for traffic on warm weekends and summer days) and head out toward the end of the point. There is a road of mostly soft sand out to the point; then just follow the shoreline, either close to the water, where it is mostly large, smooth rock on this point, or higher up, where you're walking on rocks and sand. Higher up is brushier, and many of the plants there have stickers that cling to fur.

After rounding the point, you trace the edge of a small inlet. About a mile from the boat ramp, you will be above where the water reaches and can cross over to follow the edge of the next point. This may require a bit of a scramble down a slope at the very last, and the crossing may be muddy if it has rained or the lake has been lowered recently (not that your dog is likely to mind a little cool mud under paw). Hike around this point and on to the next, wider one to the park boundary, about a half mile or three-quarters of a mile from the crossing on the inlet, depending on the lake level—the lower the lake, the longer the shoreline, but at lower levels you can cut across the inlets, too. Then retrace your steps.

Hikers and their pooches can hike the rocky shoreline of Lake Travis in Arkansas Bend Park.

There are stretches where the shore is quite rocky and may be hard on your dog's paws, so look for sandy surfaces, grass, and flat, smooth rocks for relief. A cooling dip into the lake water always feels good, too. Just be careful, as the shore often drops off quickly. You may see a great blue heron or other shorebirds on the hike. On the way back, you can head uphill to the campground under the trees and cut across the point, or walk back around the edge of it again.

10. Inks Lake State Park

Distance: 4.7-mile loop
Hiking time: 2.5 hours
Difficulty: Moderate
High point: 1067 feet
Elevation gain: 167 feet
Best hiking season: Year-round
Regulations: Dogs must be on leash; scoop and pack out waste; do not feed wildlife
Map: *Inks Lake State Park Hiking Trail Guide*
Contact: Inks Lake State Park, 512-793-2223, *www.tpwd.state.tx.us/park/inks*

Getting there: Take State Highway 29 west from Burnet 9 miles to the turnoff for Park Road 4. From there, it is 3 miles to the park entrance.

Notes: Entrance fee. Restrooms and water fountains at the park headquarters next to the trailhead parking lot. A park store carries snacks, drinks, film, and other items. This state park also has tent and RV camping, mini cabins, and picnic and swimming areas. The lake generally maintains a constant level and is popular for fishing, boating, water skiing, and scuba diving.

This hike combines three separate loops for a longer route with a variety of scenery and trail. Start at the parking area for the Pecan Flats Trail and amphitheater, just past the park entrance. The first half mile or so is crushed granite surface with some scrambling over granite outcroppings, alternating open areas and shade. Sharp-eyed hikers will see game trails off to either side, which give dogs plenty to sniff, and glimpses of Inks Lake to your right. Follow signs and paint markers for the Green Trail to the first turnoff, to the left, onto the Pecan Flats Trail. This crosses Park Road 4, follows a short stretch of gravel road to a parking area, then becomes

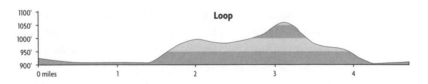

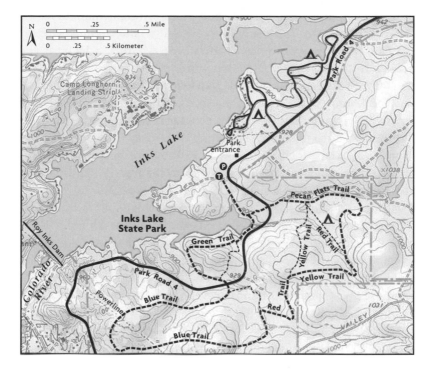

crushed granite again. The trail heads into a wooded area of tall cedars and pecans, where the smell of cedar is heavy on the air. Scattered among the trees are primitive campsites and a restroom. This is the Pecan Flats Trail Camp, for which this loop is named.

Once past the campground, the trail follows a large granite ridge. At the end of it, stay to the left to follow the Yellow Trail, rather than taking a Red Trail shortcut to the right. The trail becomes a narrow, winding track with some rising and falling and occasional scrambles over rough rock. If your dog has tender feet, or the sun is hot, you may want to use dog booties on this trail. As the route goes uphill, take a moment to stop and look back for panoramic views of the countryside, and be prepared in case you round a corner and startle a deer or two, even in broad daylight. All along the route may be coyote scat, owl pellets, and other signs of wildlife that will likely prove interesting to your hiking companion.

At the next intersection, turn left and take this Red Trail shortcut to the Blue Trail. The surface becomes quite rocky, but these are pretty rocks, and you wind among large boulders covered with a variety of mosses in interesting patterns. Tiny yellow flowers grow along and on the trail much of the year, and there are usually butterflies flitting about and lizards zipping out of sight. Shade and open areas alternate, and many of the open areas offer nice views. Then the trail enters a thick cedar break and a streambed that is full of cattails but is little more than isolated puddles most of the year. For about 50 yards, you follow a maintenance road, then head back into the trees. Where the shortcut meets the Blue Trail, turn left to follow this loop clockwise. Stretches of the Blue Trail are sand and dirt through cedar and oaks, alternating with rocky open areas.

In places where the trail crosses rock, watch for boulders lining the route and color markers to help you stick to the trail. Avoid wandering about on the rock because your feet cause erosion and also wear away the fragile plant life growing on the granite. About a half mile farther along, the trail goes under a powerline, where you have views of the lake and hills, then through more trees, several grassy areas, and over some rocky scrambles with steep twists and turns; watch closely for the markers. Pass under the powerline a second time, then through more rocky areas, some requiring a bit of jumping up and down the rocks, to another intersection. Straight ahead takes you the rest of the way around the Blue Trail loop, but turn left at a fork to cross Park Road 4 again and hook up with the Green Trail. You can turn left at the next intersection to make the longer Green Trail loop, or turn right to head over rock and down to the lake. If

The trail at Inks Lake State Park wanders through jumbles of the area's trademark pink granite.

you choose the latter, turn right again where you connect again with the Green Trail loop. There is a stretch right along the water here, and you can let your dog get a drink and cool off. Just be aware that the shore drops off quickly, especially important if your dog cannot swim.

From here, the trail follows along the shore, through tall trees and grass and over a bridge, then back to where you turned off for the Pecan Flats Trail on your way in. Backtrack along this part of the Green Trail to return to the parking lot.

11. Canyon of the Eagles, Peacock and Juniper Ridge Loops

Distance: 2.8-mile loop
Hiking time: 2.5 hours
Difficulty: Moderate to difficult
High point: 1300 feet
Elevation gain: 250 feet
Best hiking season: Fall and winter
Regulations: Dogs must be on leash; "noisy, vicious animals" are not permitted
Map: Canyon of the Eagles Hiking Trail and Endangered/Threatened Species Map
Contact: Canyon of the Eagles, 512-756-8787, *www.canyonoftheeagles.com*

Getting there: Take State Highway 29 west from Burnet about 3 miles and turn right onto Ranch Road 2341. In 15 miles, the road dead-ends at Canyon of the Eagles Lodge and Nature Park.

Notes: Entrance fee. This trail is closed March 1 through September 30 to protect golden-cheeked warblers and black-capped vireos. The trails at

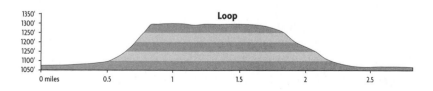

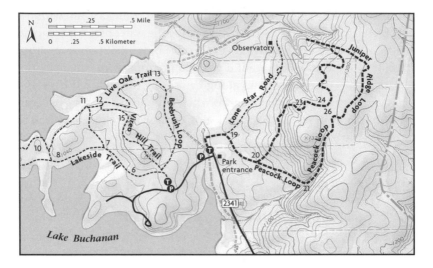

Canyon of the Eagles are well marked with a numbering system that is confusing without a map. Maps are available at the park entrance or the lodge office. This 940-acre park has campgrounds, RV sites, and sixty-four dog-friendly rooms at the lodge, which also has a swimming pool and restaurant. An observatory on the property is open for public stargazing most Wednesday and Saturday nights. A joint venture of the LCRA, with assistance from the Texas Parks and Wildlife Department and a private company, Canyon of the Eagles is home to a variety of wildlife, and some 800 acres are a nature preserve, set aside for three species of threatened or endangered birds: the American bald eagle, the black-capped vireo, and the golden-cheeked warbler. Observe the Not a Trail signs, and stay on designated trails.

This hike, which climbs a ridge to the highest point in the park affording great views of Lake Buchanan, combines the Peacock and Juniper Ridge Loops to create a longer and more scenic hike for you and your dog.

Park at the Bird and Butterfly trailhead and take an immediate right to cross a gravel road. Follow this road a short distance and turn right onto Lone Star Road, which leads to the park observatory. About 800 feet down this road, the trail leads to the right around a gate. The first part is mowed grass and packed dirt following a fence on your right and a lot of prickly pear on the left. Walk about two-tenths of a mile to marker 20, where you will reconnect after completing the loop. For now, continue straight ahead, as the trail narrows and begins to steadily

Panoramic views of Lake Buchanan and surrounding hills reward hikers who climb Juniper Ridge in Canyon of the Eagles.

rise. Watch for small cactus growing right in the trail and check paws for stickers if your dog lags or limps.

At marker 21, the trail turns left and becomes steep and rocky. But there are now trees on either side of the trail (although it is open overhead, so avoid this hike at midday), and the view behind you is ample reward for the upward scramble. On the ridge, the trail is mostly grass with scattered rocks. Enjoy the sighing of the junipers (often called cedars) in the breeze and, depending on the season, the brilliant yellow flowers or bright red fruit of the abundant prickly pear. Continue straight or bear right at markers 22, 25, and 26, where the Peacock Loop becomes the Juniper Ridge Loop, which traverses the high ground then becomes a narrow, brushy, and somewhat uneven surface zigging and zagging along the ridge. Look for glimpses of blue water between the trees. You may startle deer or even wild pigs, so have a good hold on the leash, too.

The route enters an area of denser trees and briefly becomes a bit harder to follow, so watch carefully. For about a half mile, this is the kind of trail many hikers dream of: not so much a trail as a track, barely improved, natural and rugged, and remote enough that most cell phones will not have a signal. At marker 24, turn right toward marker 23, where the trail becomes a bit more civilized again and starts to descend from the ridge through tall trees. Stay to the right at marker 23 and continue down to marker 20, where you close your loop. If it is late afternoon, you and your dog are likely to hear and spot armadillos along the gravel road and perhaps wild turkeys or even an owl.

12. Canyon of the Eagles, Beebrush, Live Oak, and Vireo Hill Trails

Distance: 2.2-mile loop
Hiking time: 1.25 hours
Difficulty: Moderate
High point: 1125 feet
Elevation gain: 100 feet
Best hiking season: Fall and winter
Regulations: Dogs must be on leash; "noisy, vicious animals" are not permitted
Map: Canyon of the Eagles Hiking Trail and Endangered/ Threatened Species Map
Contact: Canyon of the Eagles, 512-756-8787, *www.canyonoftheeagles.com*

Getting there: Take State Highway 29 west from Burnet about 3 miles and turn right onto Ranch Road 2341. In 15 miles, the road dead-ends at Canyon of the Eagles Lodge and Nature Park.

Notes: Entrance fee. Portions of this trail are closed March 1 through September 30 to protect golden-cheeked warblers and black-capped

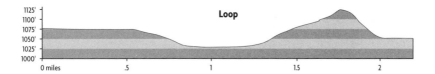

vireos. There are restrooms, water, and showers across from trailhead parking. The trails at Canyon of the Eagles are well marked with a numbering system that is confusing without a map. Maps are available at the park entrance or the lodge office. This 940-acre park has campgrounds, RV sites, and sixty-four dog-friendly rooms at the lodge, which also has a swimming pool and restaurant. An observatory on the property is open for public stargazing most Wednesday and Saturday nights. A joint venture of the LCRA, with assistance from the Texas Parks and Wildlife Department and a private company, Canyon of the Eagles is home to a variety of wildlife, and some 800 acres are a nature preserve, set aside for three species of threatened or endangered birds: the American bald eagle, the black-capped vireo, and the golden-cheeked warbler. Observe the Not a Trail signs and stay on designated trails.

Park in the amphitheater parking lot and follow the crushed granite surface to the entrance to Beebrush Loop, and head to the right. The trail, a mix of dirt and mowed brush, follows a fence that closes off the endangered bird habitat for part of the year. There are likely to be stickery plants here, so you may want to slip on your dog's booties, or check his paws frequently.

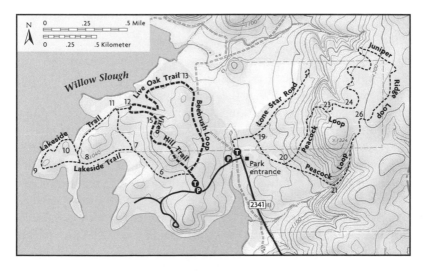

Rugged Hill Country landscape surrounds the Vireo Hill Trail in Canyon of the Eagles.

You and your dog may encounter grasshoppers launching themselves from the ground like tiny quail, as well as butterflies, dragonflies, and many birds. Other common sights are the scat of coyote and other animals, busy ants, and colorful rocks. Continue straight, or bear right, at markers 18, 17, and 14. You are now at Live Oak Junction; follow arrows to marker 13. The majority of the route is mostly sunny, with isolated shade from trees, while gentle rises punctuate this side of the loop. When you reach marker 13, turn left to follow the lakeshore for a while on a narrower and more wooded trail of softer grass. Your dog will find a lot of rotting logs and game trails offering interesting scents, and you can catch glimpses of Lake Buchanan, although thick brush makes it inaccessible. Thick piles of dead brush mark past flood levels.

Stay to the left at marker 12 for another stretch of crisp mowed grass. Turn right at marker 15 onto the Vireo Hill Trail, a narrower track that begins to climb, you guessed it, Vireo Hill. There will be some up and down, and up again, through the high point of the hill at 1125 feet, until you descend to intersect with the way you came in, Beebrush Loop, at marker 18. Follow that back to the trail to the parking lot.

13. Canyon of the Eagles, Lakeside Trail

Distance: 2.5-mile loop
Hiking time: 1.25 hours
Difficulty: Easy
High point: 1025 feet
Elevation gain: 25 feet
Best hiking season: March through June, October
Regulations: Dogs must be on leash; "noisy, vicious animals" are
  not permitted
Map: Canyon of the Eagles Hiking Trail and Endangered/Threatened
  Species Map
Contact: Canyon of the Eagles, 512-756-8787,
  www.canyonoftheeagles.com

Getting there: Take State Highway 29 west from Burnet about 3 miles and turn right onto Ranch Road 2341. In 15 miles, the road dead-ends at Canyon of the Eagles Lodge and Nature Park.

Notes: Entrance fee. Portions of this trail are closed November 1 through March 15 to protect American bald eagles. The trails at Canyon of the Eagles are well marked with a numbering system that is confusing without a map. Maps are available at the park entrance or the lodge office. This 940-acre park has campgrounds, RV sites, and sixty-four dog-friendly rooms at the lodge, which also has a swimming pool and restaurant. An observatory on the property is open for public stargazing most Wednesday and Saturday nights. A joint venture of the LCRA, with

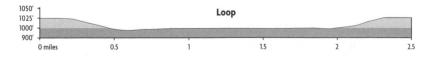

The Lakeside Trail in Canyon of the Eagles skirts close to the waters of Lake Buchanan.

assistance from the Texas Parks and Wildlife Department and a private company, Canyon of the Eagles is home to a variety of wildlife, and some 800 acres are a nature preserve, set aside for three species of threatened or endangered birds: the American bald eagle, the black-capped vireo, and the golden-cheeked warbler. Observe the Not a Trail signs and stay on designated trails.

This hike starts at the amphitheater parking lot, as does Hike 12, the Beebrush, Live Oak, and Vireo Hill Trails, but heads left toward the lake where the other hike goes right. A crushed granite surface heads through the brush, where it turns into mostly dirt, rock, and grass winding through open meadow. Views of the hills and Lake Buchanan appear, along with encounters with grasshoppers galore and dozens of dragonflies.

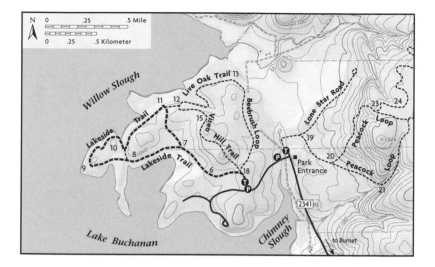

Stay to the right at markers 4 and 6, then turn left at marker 7 and again at marker 8. The trail remains in the open for about seven-tenths of a mile then, at marker 9, turns to follow the lakeshore and head into the woods. If you look up into the trees, you will likely find cactus sprouting right out of branches, sure evidence that birds eat cactus fruit. The soft dirt surface, shade, and breeze off the lake will have you and your dog lingering on this stretch. Listen for the sound of waves on the shore. At about 1.3 miles, there is access to the water so your dog can get a drink and cool his paws, and you can enjoy the wind on your face.

Continue on the trail through the open area with scattered trees, over some patches of rocky ground, and look for small bones on the trail where herons and other fish-eating birds have dined. You may hear their squawks from the water. Turn right at marker 11 to pass through an open area with good views of the tree-covered Vireo Hill, which you may have climbed on another hike. At marker 7, you close your loop and retrace your steps past markers 6 and 4 to the granite trail and back to where you parked.

AUSTIN LOW COUNTRY

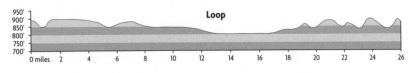

14. Lake Georgetown, Good Water Trail

Distance: 26-mile loop
Hiking time: 15 hours
Difficulty: Difficult
High point: 900 feet
Elevation gain: 160 feet
Best hiking season: Year-round
Regulations: Dogs must be on leash; pedestrian traffic only on the south side of the lake; bicycles are permitted on the north side; pack out all dog waste and trash; do not disturb plants, animals, artifacts, historical structures, or rocks
Map: Good Water Trail
Contact: U.S. Army Corps of Engineers, Georgetown Lake Office, 512-930-5253, *www.swf.usace.army.mil*

Getting there: Take Interstate 35 north from Austin and exit 261A in Georgetown. Turn left at the exit onto Williams Drive (Farm to Market Road 2338) and continue through town to D. B. Wood Drive. Turn left and follow this road past the dam to the turnoff into Cedar Breaks Park. For the Jim Hogg trailhead, stay on Williams Drive and turn left on Jim Hogg Road, which dead-ends into the park. To get to the Russell Park trailhead, continue on Williams Drive to Farm to Market Road 3405. Turn left and follow Farm to Market Road 3405 to Country Road 262. Turn left and follow CR 262 into Russell Park. The parking area and trailhead are on the right. To get to the Tejas Camp trailhead, continue down Farm to Market Road 3405 to CR 258 and turn left.

Notes: Camping is allowed in designated areas, which include primitive Cedar Hollow, Walnut Springs, and Sawyer Camps (free); Tejas Park, with water and toilets; and Cedar Breaks and Jim Hogg, with full services. Check in and out with gate attendants. The Good Water Trail is accessible from 6:00 AM to 10:00 PM at Cedar Breaks and Jim Hogg Parks; 6:00 AM to dark at Russell Park; 6:00 AM to dark at Overlook, Stilling Basin, and Booty's Road; and twenty-four hours a day at Tejas Camp. Time your hike to spend the night at one of the camps, or choose a start and end point and arrange for transportation between the two. Good Water Trail crosses the Hunt Hollow Wildlife Management area, so exercise caution during deer hunting season (stay on the trail and wear bright clothing, a must for humans and not a bad idea for dogs, too). Check with the office for hunting season dates. Cell phone service is generally good all along the trail, and carrying one is recommended in case of emergencies.

The rugged Good Water Trail is named for the Tonkawa people, or Tickanwatic, who called this land near the North Fork of the San Gabriel River the "land of good water." The trail winds through dense juniper stands, hardwood bottomlands, and prairie grasslands, often along the limestone cliffs that border Lake Georgetown, which was constructed by the Corps of Engineers for flood control. The lake also serves as the water supply for Georgetown and Round Rock. Drinking water for hikers is available only at Overlook, Cedar Breaks, Jim Hogg, and Tejas, so carry adequate water.

The trail makes a complete loop around the lake, with several options for overnight camping or for shorter hikes, if you arrange transportation between start and end points.

From Russell Park to Cedar Breaks, markers are posted at 1-mile intervals (counting upward clockwise), although some are missing or obscured, and occasional hiking trail markers or camp signs help you determine your whereabouts. In general, on the route given here, keep the lake on your left and you won't get far off track.

This route begins at Cedar Breaks and covers the entire route going counterclockwise. However, the first 1.3 miles are on asphalt road across

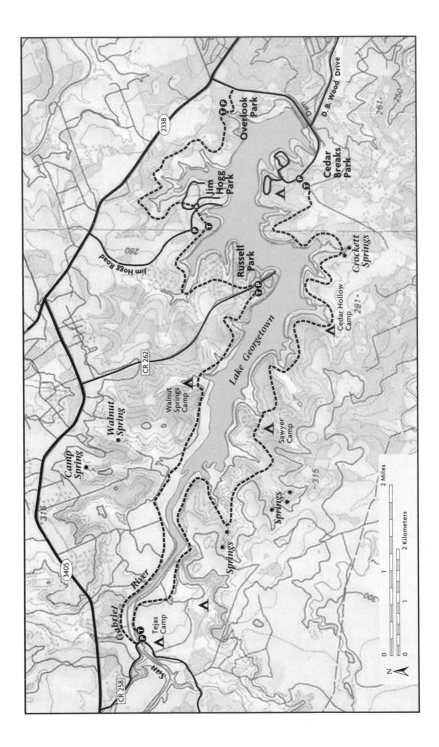

the dam; if you are going to make the entire loop, but want to avoid this stretch, leave your car at Cedar Breaks and have someone drop you and your dog off at Overlook Park, off D. B. Wood Road. At Overlook Park, find the trail at the end of the parking lot to the right of a sidewalk that leads to the restrooms and picnic area. If you are planning a shorter hike, you can choose beginning and ending points that avoid the dam. From Overlook Park, the surface is initially crushed granite, bending right and becoming a rocky double track. About 75 yards after this bend, follow a narrow trail that turns left into the trees (do not continue straight on the double track). The rocky dirt trail winds through open brush and shady areas, tracing the distant lakeshore before winding away from the water to circumnavigate an inlet. You then head back toward the main body of the lake, through areas of large trees as well as open spaces. Some of the time, the lake water will be visible in the distance. Deer are abundant here, as are birds, and your dog will find plenty of interesting scents.

After hiking through an open area, you will cross a stream and wind through more trees before reaching Jim Hogg Park. Pick up the trail across the road just past the entrance booth (there are restrooms and water inside this park, if you need them). You will be following a narrow dirt track that quickly becomes rocky and rugged, winding through junipers. The lake is briefly visible through the trees on your right before a switchback puts it back on your left and the trail roughly follows the shore, which is well below you. There is some scrambling over rock here and roots across the trail. The only markers are orange plastic streamers, but the trail is quite obvious in this section. Listen for birds, including woodpeckers, in a stand of taller trees, then cross a rocky drainage and an open area dotted with cactus. You and your dog will wind through more woods, then down and across a gurgling stream. Just after you cross, there is a short detour to the right to see the stream cascading into a deep pool where you can spot little fish.

Continue through alternating open and wooded areas and up and down rocky slopes that will require an occasional jump by smaller dogs and along a hillside before heading over a small ridge into heavier woods. You will cross another stream, then follow the trail along a bluff high above the lake. Look for an old stone wall, now little more than a slightly organized jumble of moss-covered rocks. The trail splits, although the two parts quickly rejoin.

The trail eventually winds away from the bluff, around an inlet and a rocky drainage, winding around a bit more before emerging in Russell

Jenny and Sierra cross a creek on their way to Tejas Camp on the Good Water Trail.

Park. You will cross an asphalt road and meander through the trees, crossing another park road just past the entrance, before reaching a parking area for the Russell Park trailhead.

Leaving Russell Park, the rocky, dirt trail twists and turns through juniper woods with some up and down, then, after about 2 miles, heads down closer to the lakeshore and into open grassland, where you will be walking on a dirt road. You will see a lot of flood debris along the trail and lakeshore, as well as some stretches of old barbed wire fencing, and are likely to encounter deer. There are patches of large trees to provide occasional shade as the road heads gradually uphill. Look for an old stone wall nearly obscured by overgrowth on the left and, at one point, a flowing creek on your right. You will also see houses high on the hills off to the right, just outside the park boundary. Eventually, the trail veers away from the lake and through fields of tall grass. Birds, mice, and other creatures rustling in the grass will likely catch your dog's interest. Just remember to keep him on the trail. A concrete low-water bridge, the old Hunt Crossing, is visible off to the left, with a trail leading down to it, but your turnoff is a bit farther. Look for a trail to the left leading away from the dirt road, and a hiker trail sign a few yards beyond the turnoff. This takes you down steps to cross a small creek, up the other bank, and through another grassy field before descending close to the San Gabriel River at the far end of the lake. You follow the river for a short way before crossing a bridge on the road into Tejas Camp. This is a good spot to take a break, or to camp overnight.

You leave the area on a mostly dirt trail under tall trees along the river, then turn onto a wide, mowed route through the grasses toward hills. There are several narrower trails in this area, but they all head in the same direction; just keep the lake on the left and you will be fine. On the other side of the fields, a cliff rises on your right and an old fence is on the left. Before long, steps take you up this cliff to follow the edge of the tree-covered ridge above the clear, blue water of the lake. Between mile markers 10 and 8 are more open fields, and at one point, the trail turns away from the lake to head along an inlet up to a crossing point. After the crossing, the trail follows the top of a long, low levy, where armadillos are a frequent sight. Then it goes up a steep, rocky hill, crests it, and descends to Sawyer Camp, about halfway between mile markers 7 and 6. You head back into trees and more climbing on loose rock, where you will need to pay attention to keep track of the trail. Just after passing another hiker trail sign and stepping over a big black pipe, you cross a dirt road to pick up the trail on the other side, along the earthen dam forming a pretty pond that is likely to have ducks swimming in it. At the end of the dam, you head up a steep hill, winding through interesting, pockmarked boulders. The trail goes up and down the rocky hills here, crossing uneven ground and rocks of a variety of shapes and colors. Follow a rock shelf around a wash and along the top of a cliff above the water. The junipers are thick in this area, as are the prickly pear cactus, with the two sometimes growing so close together that you must squeeze between them. Watch your step and take care to avoid getting cactus spines in your shins, but be careful about sharp twigs at face level as well. Two wooden bridges traverse narrow washes, one of them quite deep and usually filled with water. Between mileposts 3 and 2 is a parcel of land occupied by a succession of settlers, who left behind a number of artifacts. The trail crosses a pool decked with elephant ears, an exotic plant species introduced by one of the owners. This pool is formed by the flow from Crockett Springs, which feeds a waterfall to your left. There is a short detour at the bottom of the hill that takes you below the falls. This is an environmentally sensitive area, so stay on the trail and keep your dog out of the water. Back on the main trail, you will head up another draw, through an old corral (a historical structure), and over another spring flow. Once again, you ascend to the top of the cliffs and follow the lakeshore along very rocky, moonscapelike ground, through more junipers and cactus. The next mile turns away from the lake, winding through trees and over rocks to the Cedar Breaks trailhead parking area.

15. Bastrop State Park, Lost Pines Trail

Distance: 8.2-mile loop
Hiking time: 3.5 hours
Difficulty: Moderate
High point: 572 feet
Elevation gain: 165 feet
Best hiking season: Year-round
Regulations: Dogs must be on leash; hike on marked trails only; no bicycles allowed on the trails; overnight camping permitted east of the old roadbed—camp 50 feet from the trail and 100 feet from open water; no ground fires allowed
Map: Bastrop State Park Lost Pines Hiking Trail
Contact: Bastrop State Park, 512-321-2101, *www.tpwd.state.tx.us/park/bastrop*

Getting there: From Austin, take State Highway 71 east to Bastrop, turn left on State Highway 21, which bears right in about a quarter mile. The park is about a mile up the hill on the right.

Notes: Entrance fee. The park has picnic areas, campsites, cabins, lodges, and a swimming pool with a bathhouse built by the Civilian Conservation Corps. In addition to the Lost Pines Trail, there are another 3.5 miles of hiking trails. White-tailed deer, rabbits, squirrels, opossums, and armadillos live in the woods, as do many species of birds. Bird checklists are available at park headquarters.

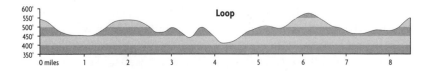

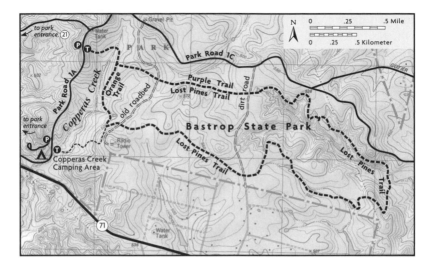

Bastrop State Park is part of the "Lost Pines," an area of loblolly pine and hardwoods separated from the East Texas Pineywoods by about 100 miles of rolling post oak woodlands. Considered the most westerly stand of loblolly pines in the United States, the area covers about 70 square miles. After entering the park, turn left onto Park Road 1A and follow it around the cabin area, lake, and the intersection with Park Road 1C, a scenic drive to nearby Buescher State Park. Continue on Park Road 1A to the scenic overlook and Lost Pines trailhead on your right, not far past the intersection. The Lost Pines Trail makes a loop from here or another trailhead farther down Park Road 1A by the Copperas Creek Camping Area (if you are camping, you can walk to that trailhead from the campground).

From the scenic overlook parking area, the pine-needle–covered path plunges immediately into tall pines and heads downhill. Most of the route is quite shady, and the surface is typically rock and sand, in some places so fine and deep that walking is challenging for those with two legs. The trail is marked with brown posts with purple decals, indicating the Lost Pines Trail, and metal rectangles fastened onto trees, with their position indicating the direction the route goes. There are trail maps posted at each junction. The first cross trail you come to, at about four-tenths of a mile, is the Orange Trail, which continues straight ahead to the south Lost Pines (Purple) Trail, returning to Park Road 1A near Copperas Creek Camping Area (you will be coming back that way). Follow the Purple Trail as it veers to the left. You and your dog will be hiking over gently undulating, wooded hills, passing moss-covered trunks and fallen logs, which sometimes lie across the path. Dogs will find plenty to sniff, while humans listen to the distinctive sound of wind through pines and the calls of birds.

You will cross an old roadbed (camping is allowed east of this) and pass a pond. You will notice signs of burning on trees where the park staff has conducted prescribed burns to reduce dangerous fuel loads, increase the diversity of vegetation, and improve the overall habitat in the forest. About a mile farther, the route crosses a dirt road, Harmon Road, and skirts another pond. The trail heads down a slope of loose rock, then winds along the side of a hill before taking a steep plunge down the slope, followed by a steep uphill stretch.

Just before mile 3, you cross under a powerline, then the trail winds about and rises and falls, crossing a creekbed ten or eleven times. The creek is generally dry, and there are stepping-stones for crossing when water is flowing. After working your way back uphill, you will cross under the powerlines again, then through a small meadow and past several ponds, then once again over the dirt road. Continue winding through the trees, keeping an eye out for trail markers. There is a bench just before the trail crosses the old roadbed and heads downhill and then up, passing a low ledge of weathered boulders. At the intersection, turn right onto the Orange Trail (straight ahead takes you to the trailhead near the Copperas

Fallen logs on the Lost Pines Trail make the hike interesting for Max.

Creek Camping Area). Fallen pine needles cover the thick brush here to create an eerie atmosphere. The needles also form a thick carpet on many parts of the trail. It is about six-tenths of a mile along the Orange Trail before it meets the main trail you came in on. Head left, up a long slope back to where you parked.

16. Lake Bastrop South Shore Park

Distance: 2.5-mile loop
Hiking time: 1.25 hours
Difficulty: Easy
High point: 480 feet
Elevation gain: 20 feet
Best hiking season: Year-round
Regulations: Dogs must be on leash
Map: USGS Lake Bastrop 7.5' Quadrangle
Contact: Lower Colorado River Authority, Lake Bastrop Administrative Office, 512-303-7666, *www.lcra.org/community/southshore.html*

Getting there: From Austin, take State Highway 71 east to Bastrop. Turn left onto State Highway 95, then right onto State Highway 21. About 2 miles farther, turn left onto County Road 352/South Shore Road and drive 1.4 miles to the park entrance, which is marked. After entering the park, turn right toward the camping area and take the first right to the trail parking lot.

Notes: Day-use entrance fee. Hours change seasonally, so call ahead. General park information is at *www.lcra.org*. The South Shore Park has campsites with electricity and cabins (although pets are not allowed in cabins). Reservations for camping can be made through the Texas Parks and Wildlife central reservation system, Monday through Friday, 9:00 AM to 6:00 PM, at 512-389-8900. The South Shore administrative office, near the boat ramp, is open Monday through Friday, 8:00 AM to 5:00 PM.

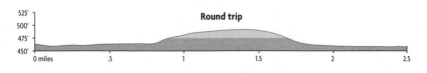

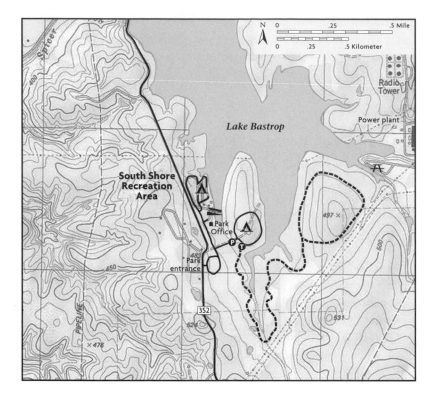

A hiking trail on the south side of the park winds through woods and around part of Lake Bastrop, with a loop at the end. There are metal tags marking the trail, although not many, but the trail is well defined and easy to follow. Shortly after leaving the parking area, the trail forks, with the left fork leading to the lakeshore. Since you will not be hiking along the water, take a minute to detour here and get a good look at the pretty lake. Then retrace your steps back to the trail and continue.

The surface is dirt and sand, generally well packed, and soon becomes a double track. You and your four-legged companion will be winding through pine and juniper stands, thick brush, and some small open fields. The route then follows a barbed wire fence for a short distance, passes a gate, and tramps through a thick stand of brush. At the end of this, it veers left; a narrow trail appears to continue straight, but stick with the double track. After more winding through the trees, you will see the lake ahead and, as the trail veers to the right away from it, there is another short detour to the shore. A little farther along, the trail forks and a post points in both directions. This is a loop, so head whichever

The tranquil shore of Lake Bastrop is a scenic place to rest after hiking at South Shore Park.

way you fancy, or let your dog choose. There are open areas, large stands of oak, and plenty of pine trees, and you will see signs of animals, most likely armadillos, rooting in the pine-needle–covered ground. Complete the loop and then retrace your steps back to the parking lot.

17. Buescher State Park

Distance: 7.7-mile balloon loop
Hiking time: 3.5 hours
Difficulty: Moderate
High point: 490 feet
Elevation gain: 110 feet
Best hiking season: Year-round
Regulations: Dogs must be on leash; stay on designated trails; no overnight camping on trail; pets are not allowed in cabins or screened shelters
Map: Buescher Hiking Trail 7.7-Mile Route
Contact: Buescher State Park, 512-237-2241, *www.tpwd.state.tx.us/park/buescher*

Getting there: Take State Highway 71 east from Austin through Bastrop toward Smithville. Turn left (north) onto Farm to Market Road 153. The

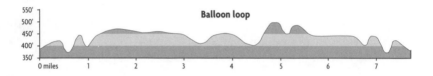

park entrance is about a half mile farther on your left. After you check in at the park entrance, proceed on Park Road 1E past two turnoffs for picnic areas (there are restrooms and water here), a recreation hall, and a campground to the parking lot for the walk-in campsites, which is also parking for the trailhead. The trailhead is across the park road from the parking lot and has an information kiosk and several picnic tables.

Notes: Entrance fee. The park has multiuse and tent camping, picnic areas, a recreation hall, and a playground, in addition to a lake that allows nonmotorized boating and fishing for catfish, bass, crappie, perch, and, in the winter, rainbow trout.

Buescher State Park is on beautiful, wooded land, part of the "Lost Pines," the most westerly stand of loblolly pines in the United States, a 70-square-mile area of pine and hardwoods separated from the East Texas Pineywoods by about 100 miles of rolling post oak woodlands. This land was part of Stephen F. Austin's original colonial grant, and the El Camino Real or King's Highway, which connected San Antonio de Bexar (now the city of San Antonio) and Spanish missions in east Texas, passed near the park along what is present-day State Highway 21 and Old San Antonio Road. Original park improvements were made by the Civilian Conservation Corps, and CCC-built facilities are still in use in the park. A scenic, 12-mile drive through the forest on Park Road 1C connects Buescher State Park and Bastrop State Park (Hike 15). If you and your dog make both hikes, you will enjoy taking this drive between them.

The first 30 yards or so of the trail are soft mulch, then the trail becomes dirt with scattered patches of rocks, often covered with leaves or pine needles. On this heavily wooded route, you will need to keep an eye out for roots across the trail, as well as fallen logs, some requiring your dog to make like Rin Tin Tin and jump. Metal tags attached to the trees, with position indicating trail direction, mark the route, along with signs at intersections. The trail falls and rises gently in this first half mile, follows a creekbed for a ways and then crosses it, winding through more moss-covered trees and thick brush. Then you emerge onto an open, grassy pipeline right-of-way, walking downhill and up for 0.4 mile, passing close to the park road and crossing a trickling stream before turning back into the trees. You and your dog then wind through more woods, ascending and descending and passing a drainage and an old roadbed. Dogs will find plenty of interesting scents along this pine-shaded trail, and their owners may spot some of the 250-odd species of birds that are in the park seasonally. A birding checklist is available in the park office.

You cross a paved road that leads to the University of Texas Science Park, a research facility occupying about 700 acres, which were originally part of the park then deeded to the university's M. D. Anderson Cancer Center. The trail swings close to some of those facilities, which are closed to visitors, and you may hear noise from the center for a short while on

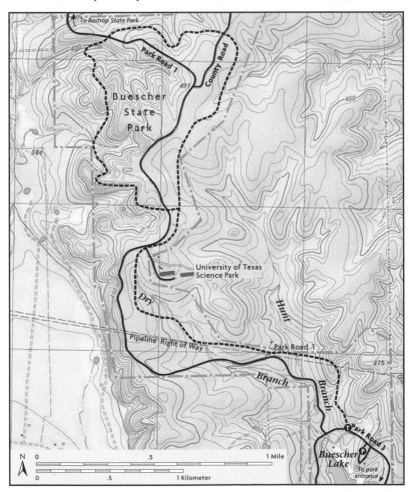

Sharp-eyed hikers can find treasures like this bird's nest near the trail in Buescher State Park.

the trail. You may also hear some traffic on the park road and private airplanes landing or taking off from a small airport in Smithville, just a few miles away. Otherwise, for most of the hike, the sound of the wind through pines and the calls of birds will be all you hear. Look for reindeer lichen, green mosslike plants growing low to the ground among the trees, as well as lichens on fallen logs and mushrooms growing in the soft ground. Pinecones, of course, are scattered everywhere, and you may even see an occasional bird's nest that has fallen from a tree. The trail skirts a pond, then becomes a bit rockier as it passes through an area with fewer pine trees and more junipers. You emerge on a dirt road, from which the trail goes both ways. To the left is a connecting trail that allows you to shorten the route by a little more than a mile. To make the full 7.7-mile route, turn right.

The narrow trail crosses and then follows a streambed, which is usually dry. Pine trees once again dominate, and if there is wind you can hear strange creaks, groans, and even a buglelike sound made by trees rubbing together. You cross the streambed again, wind around and then cross a paved county road. After this, the trail drops down and traces the edge of a deep drainage, where the brush is draped in pine needles. The route descends, crosses another drainage, then goes steeply down and up to cross another one. The footing here, on sand and pine needles, can be a bit tricky. There may be downed logs across the path here, too, that your dog can jump. After crossing the park road again, the trail wanders down the side of a hill, then drops more steeply into a drainage, crosses it, and heads back up. You follow the edge of a deep wash for a ways, then go down and cross it. Then the trail intersects with the end of the shortcut that you passed on the other side of the loop. Turn right to continue the loop.

You follow the course of a drainage near the bottom for a while, then the trail rises, dips back down, and crosses it, passing through spooky, pine-needle–draped brush. You continue along the bottom of the wash, then over a wooden bridge before winding around and climbing up and out. There is another crossing of the park road, which is an opportunity to cut your hike short if you've arranged a pickup. In a short distance, the loop closes and you will be retracing your steps for 2.2 miles. In these hills and thick woods, though, everything looks different from the other direction, so you and your dog will still enjoy this part.

This trail is scheduled for clearing and new markers, improvements that may be completed in 2006.

18. McKinney Falls State Park, Homestead Trail

Distance: 3-mile loop
Hiking time: 1.5 hours
Difficulty: Easy
High point: 580 feet
Elevation gain: 80 feet
Best hiking season: Year-round
Regulations: Dogs must be on leash and are not allowed to swim in the creek
Map: Texas Parks and Wildlife McKinney Falls State Park
Contact: McKinney Falls State Park, 512-243-1643,
www.tpwd.state.tx.us/spdest/findadest/parks/mckinney_falls

Getting there: From the junction of State Highway 71 and Interstate 183 southeast of Austin, take Interstate 183 south to McKinney Falls Parkway, turn right and go 3 miles to the park entrance on your right. From the entrance, take the first right, following signs to the picnic area. Park at the end of this road.

Notes: Entrance fee. There are restrooms at the picnic area, along with picnic tables and a playground, and more restrooms next to the parking area for the trailhead. There is water for your dog at the restrooms and from the creek but not along the trail. The park also has campsites, including walk-in sites, screened shelters, and an interpretive center. There is also a 3-mile paved trail that loops around the main area, past Upper McKinney Falls and along Onion Creek.

From the parking area, take the gravel road a short distance through the trees to a large expanse of open rock, which may be hot on the paws in summer. Ahead is Onion Creek, which you will cross, an easy task most of the year but not after heavy rains (check creek conditions by calling the park ahead of time). Your pup can get a drink here, but isn't allowed

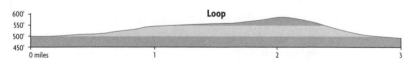

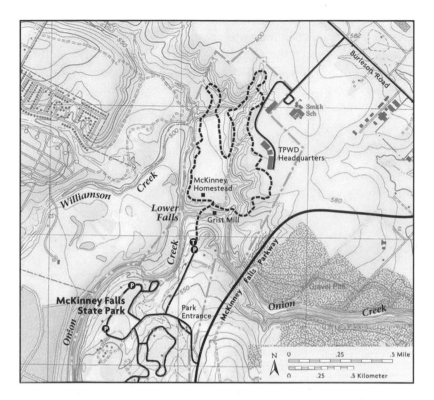

to swim in the creek. You're crossing just above the Lower Falls, so watch your step. On the other side, the trailhead is to your right and marked as Homestead Trail. This trail alternates dirt, dirt with scattered rock, and rocky surface and is mostly shady with some open areas, mostly in the second half of the loop.

Follow the trail into the thick brush here and bear left at the ruins of the homestead of Thomas McKinney, one of Stephen F. Austin's first three hundred colonists. McKinney settled on this property sometime around 1850. The sun-dappled hike and bike trail winds through trees and brush, rising and falling just a bit. You are likely to hear various wild creatures rustling in the brush, along with the sharp chirrups of cardinals, and your dog will pick up on a lot of interesting scents. Look for bushes with tiny red berries, prickly pear, beetles on the trail, and spiderwebs. The trail twists and turns a lot and crosses a maintenance road twice in this first half of the loop. Then it becomes more rocky and open, rising and falling a bit more, and passing close to a road, which you'll likely be able to hear before you see it. At the far side of the loop, the trail passes next to a Texas Parks and Wildlife building, then follows a maintenance road for a few yards before reentering the trees and crossing a wooden bridge. A rocky stretch through trees, including an impressive motte of cedars, leads into a grassy open area overlooked by the parks department headquarters (but of course your dog will be on her leash!).

Onion Creek has cut interesting shapes into the limestone in McKinney Falls State Park.

You then pass a very impressive oak, go down and across a dry wash, through a stand of oaks, and down into a long, open stretch, where you'll cross some bedrock. There's a picnic table here, and a bit farther on you pass what's left of the homestead's old grist mill, cross more rock, and end up back where you started. Let your dog take a nice long drink and cool her paws, then head back across the rocky area and to the parking lot.

19. McKinney Roughs Nature Park, Outer Loop

Distance: 5.5 miles round trip
Hiking time: 2.75 hours
Difficulty: Moderate
High point: 550 feet
Elevation gain: 200 feet
Best hiking season: Year-round
Regulations: Dogs must be on leash; scoop and pack out waste; hikers yield to horses
Map: McKinney Roughs Trail Map
Contact: Lower Colorado River Authority, McKinney Roughs Nature Park, 512-303-5073, *www.lcra.org/community/mckinney_roughs.html*

Getting there: From Austin, take State Highway 71 east about 13 miles. The entrance to McKinney Roughs Nature Park will be on the left 8 miles west of Bastrop. Turn in and follow the drive to the parking lot by the Mark Rose Natural Science Center.

Notes: Entrance fee. Hikers are requested to check in and out at the park office. Trails may be closed periodically for maintenance, so call 800-776-5272, extension 7427, for current conditions. Park hours are 8:00 AM to 5:00 PM Monday through Saturday, noon to 5:00 PM Sundays; closed major holidays.

Elements of four unique ecosystems—Post Oak Savannah, Blackland Prairie, East Texas Pineywoods, and Central Texas Plateau—can be found within this 1100-acre nature park owned and operated by the Lower Colorado River Authority (LCRA). More than 15 miles of trails web the park's rolling canyons, river bottoms, and wildflower meadows, where hundreds of species of animals and birds live. This route combines portions of the

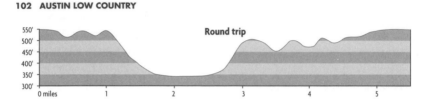

Bobcat Ridge, Coyote Road, Riverside, Cypress, and Pine Ridge Trails for an outer loop around the park.

After checking in at headquarters, take a short walk along the road to where Bobcat Ridge Trail crosses, and turn right. This trail is deep sand, well churned by hooves, through brush and then an open area. The dirt becomes more packed as the trail zigzags down a ridge to Coyote Road. Turn right onto this wide dirt and rock road, which rises and falls on its way to the river. Look for hawks flying overhead, and watch for the turnoff to the Riverside Trail on your right. Take this narrower dirt track that winds into thicker trees, and then through wooded river bottom and across a drainage. Here, the Bluestem Trail forks to the right, but you continue left to crest a rise for your first sight of the Colorado River. The

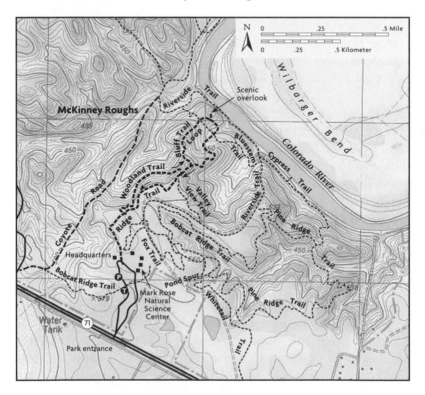

With decaying logs, piles of leaves, and an abundance of wildlife, there is plenty for dogs like Max to sniff.

trail parallels the river for about a half mile, below a bluff rising on your right and among trees alive with birds. Just past a picnic table, there is access to the water, where ducks and herons are a common sight. A short distance later, the Riverside Trail turns back toward park headquarters, but you and your dog will continue ahead, onto the Cypress Trail along the river. There is a short detour here to a watering hole for horses, which also works for dogs.

The Cypress Trail now becomes a hikers-only trail, heading up and becoming narrow and twisty. The river gurgles over some shoals here, and you may also hear cows on the other side. You will then head uphill to an intersection with the Pine Ridge Trail, where you will turn right, going up and up some more, climbing a steep slope into pine trees, and finally emerging onto the top of the ridge. Just around a bend here is a bench with spectacular views of the river, pastures, and surrounding tree-covered hills. The now-rocky trail traces this ridge for quite a ways along a steep drop-off, then wanders away from the edge through some trees, including hickories (look for nuts on the ground in the fall). It occasionally teeters on the edge again, often even with treetops, then crosses open areas where you will see cactus for the first time. There are also a number of old structures and fencing in this area.

Here, Pine Ridge Trail follows the ridgeline to the other side of a small valley where a number of very large pines grow. It then goes down into the tip of this valley, and back up, passing the Pond Spur Trail. You will scrape close to the Whitetail Trail, finally crossing it twice, coming to where the Pine Ridge, Riverside, and Fox Trails all intersect. Go straight, still on Pine Ridge, following signs to the park headquarters. You will come in on the opposite side of the building complex from where you started. There are restrooms and water faucets here.

20. McKinney Roughs Nature Park, Woodland and Bluff Ridge Trails

Distance: 2.1-mile loop
Hiking time: 1 hour
Difficulty: Moderate
High point: 550 feet
Elevation gain: 150 feet
Best hiking season: Year-round
Regulations: Dogs must be on leash; scoop and pack out waste; hikers yield to horses
Map: McKinney Roughs Trail Map
Contact: McKinney Roughs Nature Park, 512-303-5073, *www.lcra.org/community/mckinney_roughs.html*

Getting there: From Austin, take State Highway 71 east about 13 miles. The entrance to McKinney Roughs Nature Park will be on the right 8 miles west of Bastrop. Turn in and follow the drive to the parking lot by the Mark Rose Natural Science Center.

Notes: Hikers are requested to check in and out at the park office. Entrance fee. Trails may be closed periodically for maintenance, so call 800-776-5272, extension 7427, for current conditions. Park hours are

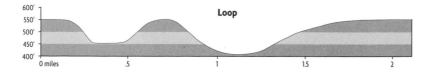

8:00 AM to 5:00 PM Monday through Saturday, noon to 5:00 PM Sundays; closed major holidays. The science center has exhibits on the animals native to the area, including a 1300-gallon aquarium filled with fish from the Colorado River (dogs are not allowed in the buildings, however).

McKinney Roughs Nature Park, owned and operated by the Lower Colorado River Authority (LCRA), has more than 15 miles of trails and elements of four distinct Texas regions: Post Oak Savannah, Blackland Prairie, East Texas Pineywoods, and Central Texas Plateau. Dozens of species of birds and a variety of wildlife, including white-tailed deer, armadillo, and gray fox, call the 1100 acres home.

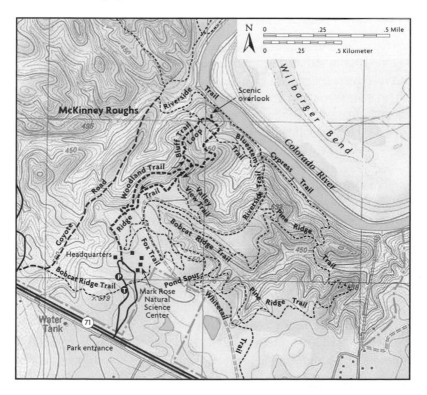

A scenic view of the Colorado River is worth a short detour at the far side of the Bluff Ridge Trail.

This route, a squished figure eight, is a shorter alternative to the Hike 19 loop, but one that still provides a good look at the Colorado River and the park's unique landscapes. It involves hiking all or parts of the Ridge Trail, Woodland Trail, and Bluff Trail Loop. Both the Ridge and Woodland Trails are compacted granite gravel and wheelchair-accessible trails, so it is especially important to clean up after your dog here. Catch the Ridge Trail behind the park headquarters complex and follow it along the top of a ridge. You will pass several observation points with benches on your left. Just past a marked wildflower meadow, turn left onto the Woodland Trail, following its switchbacks down the slope through woods that include juniper, cedar, elm, oak, and hickory trees.

More switchbacks take you back up the slope and to the other end of the Ridge Trail. Turn left here for a short walk out to an observation point, then return to the intersection and take the rocky trail down the hill. It is just a short distance to the Bluff Trail Loop; turn left. Near the other end of this loop, the Bluff Trail crosses the Bluestem Trail and there is a short, worthwhile detour to your left providing a scenic view of the river below. As you continue on the trail, several other places offer a good look at the river. You and your dog wind downhill, cross Bluestem again, and start back up. Some of the trail is rocky, and there are occasional roots across it. When you get back to the start of the loop, turn right toward park headquarters.

After a short backtrack—this is the middle of the rough figure eight that the two loops form—you will be back on the Ridge Trail. Here you will pass nice views, many of them with benches facilitating their enjoyment, and a number of wildflower meadows, before returning to the Woodland Trail turnoff and retracing your steps to the starting point.

21. Lake Somerville State Park and Trailway

Distance: 13 miles one way
Hiking time: 6.5 hours
Difficulty: Moderate
High point: 300 feet
Elevation gain: 60 feet
Best hiking season: Year-round
Regulations: Dogs must be on leash
Map: Texas Parks and Wildlife Lake Somerville State Park and Trailway
Contact: Texas Parks and Wildlife, Lake Somerville State Park,
Birch Creek Unit, 979-535-7763,
www.tpwd.state.tx.us/spdest/findadest/parks/lake_somerville

Getting there: To reach the Birch Creek Unit from Houston, take US Highway 290 northwest to Brenham, then State Highway 36 north through Somerville to Lyons. Turn left onto Farm to Market Road 60 and go about 8 miles to Park Road 57, turn right, then it's 4 miles to the park. From Austin, take US Highway 290 east to State Highway 21; turn left and drive approximately 30 miles. Turn right onto Farm to Market Road 60 and continue 11 miles to Park Road 57 and 4 miles to the park.

To reach the Nails Creek Unit from Houston, take US Highway 290 west to Burton and exit on Spur 125. Turn left onto Farm to Market Road 1697 and follow it to Farm to Market Road 180 and turn right to the

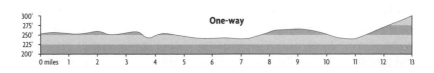

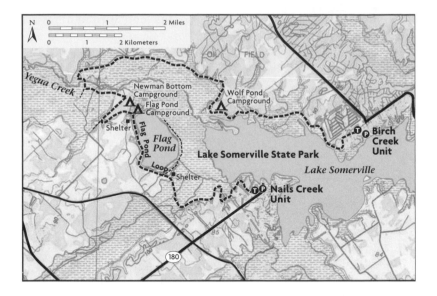

park. From Austin, take US Highway 290 east 6 miles past Giddings and turn left onto Farm to Market Road 180 to the park.

Notes: Entrance fee. Hikers share the trail with cyclists and equestrians. Stay on designated trails. Do not cross fences. Avoid oil-field equipment and drilling areas. Nonpotable water is available at Newman Bottom and Wolf Pond campsites, and all primitive camps have pit toilets. Waterfowl hunting is allowed on Flag Pond until noon on certain dates; call the park office for the schedule. There are a number of open shelters along the trail with benches, which provide good places to rest and perhaps share a treat with your dog. The shelters have trail maps and time lines that will help you see how far you have come on your hike. Birch Creek is 2365 acres and has walk-in campsites with water, equestrian campsites with water, campsites with electric and water, and a group dining hall with group campsites. There are also a picnic area, boat ramp, and fishing dock, where anglers can catch bass, crappie, and catfish. The 3155-acre Nails Creek Unit is open for day use only. The Somerville complex also includes a 3180-acre wildlife management area.

The Lake Somerville Trailway system connects the park's Birch Creek Unit on the north shore of the lake with the Nails Creek Unit on its south shore, on gently rolling terrain. It passes through dense stands of yaupon and post oak, hickory, blackjack oak, and water oak, by scenic overlooks, and over flowing streams. Impressive displays of spring wildflowers can be found along the way.

This route starts at Birch Creek. If you aren't backpacking, arrange for pickup at the Nails Creek Unit. It is about a thirty-minute drive from one place to the other. The first part of the trail, as with much of the entire distance, is a sandy double track. The sand is often soft and deep, slowing your pace, especially on hills. Stretches of loose rock are also common, and some parts of the trail are grass covered. For the most part, you and your dog are hiking in the open, so protect yourself from the sun, but there are plenty of shady spots along the way. For the first 3.5 miles, you will get occasional glimpses of the lake through the trees as the trail winds close to the shore and then away from it on the gently undulating land. Both wooded and open areas are often busy with birds, and raccoons have left tracks in the soft dirt.

Near the marker for mile 3, the trail passes through thick woods and rounds a hillside, where the woods open up and hikers can enjoy a panoramic view. One of the shelters is near here, just before mile 4 and the Wolf Pond Campground. Around mile 5, you enter a sprawling, open

Shelters along the Lake Somerville Trailway provide shade and maps to track your progress.

meadow of tall grass dotted with trees. There is a tank facility and several oil-well pumps near mile 6. The trail heads across the meadow, passing a shelter in the middle and a turnoff to several backpack camping areas. On the other side, you wind back into the trees, which often creak in the wind, then, shortly, cross Yegua Creek, which flows year-round. Construction of a dam on this creek by the U.S. Army Corps of Engineers in 1962, about 2 miles south of Somerville, created Lake Somerville. Detour along the creek banks to find access for your dog to get a drink, or rest at one of the picnic tables.

Straight ahead is a loop trail that reconnects with the main trail in 1.2 miles. Turn left to stay on the main trail, which roughly follows the creek for a while, crosses a side creek, and then traverses an open area to an intersection. The trail straight ahead leads to the Newman Bottom and Flag Pond campsites, then connects to the Flag Pond Loop Trail. Turn right to stay on the main trail, walking along the boundary between an open meadow and thick brush. After dipping down and back up, the main trail takes a sharp left and encounters stretches of small, loose rocks. The next intersection is a meeting of the Flag Pond Loop and the main route, which goes to the right. There is a shelter here where you can check the map and a time line to see how you are doing, then enjoy the view of Flag Pond, which is a water impoundment in a natural depression in the Yegua Creek watershed. Not far past here, a bird blind and covered picnic area allow a closer look at the waterfowl on the pond and the many birds in the brush (bird checklists are available at park headquarters).

The trail next passes through tall trees and thick brush and a stand of pine trees. Just over a rise you will see a line of hunting cabins on the right, which are outside the park boundary on private property (do not trespass). Continue circling the pond to another shelter at the other end, and an intersection with the other end of the loop around Flag Pond. Turn right to head for the Nails Creek Unit of Lake Sommerville State Park.

Hike through open grassland then trees to cross the actual Nails Creek near mile 11, then wind around, uphill, and down in soft dirt. Look for game trails and keep an eye out for birds. The trail continues to rise and fall, then near mile 12 you catch sight of Lake Somerville again. You will circle a tank field on your right, jumbles of rocks on the left, then wind through trees and over hills until emerging at the Nails Creek Unit. Just to the left of the end of the trail is a pavilion with restrooms and a water faucet for you and your dog. If you've arranged to be picked up here, this is a good landmark to give drivers as a place to meet.

SAN ANTONIO

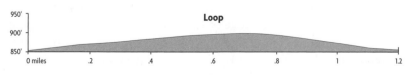

22. O. P. Schnabel Park, Leon Creek Vista

Distance: 1.2-mile loop
Hiking time: 1 hour
Difficulty: Easy to moderate
High point: 900 feet
Elevation gain: 50 feet
Best hiking season: Year-round
Regulations: Dogs must be on leash
Map: USGS Helotes 7.5' Quadrangle
Contact: San Antonio Parks and Recreation, 210-207-7275
www.sanantonio.gov/sapar

Getting there: From downtown San Antonio, take Interstate 10 west to Loop 410 west (left). From Loop 410, take the exit for State Highway 16 and turn right to the park entrance, on your right, at 9606 Bandera Road. When the park road ends, turn right to the parking area by the pavilion. This park also has a YMCA facility.

Notes: There are picnic tables, water fountains, and restrooms in the park.

This park is popular and at first seems quite urban, but it is easy to spot wildlife, even on the main, paved trail. This hike barely scratches the surface of the park's 202 acres and 4.5 miles of official trail, but the unpaved trails are not marked (and overuse has created many rogue trails), so it is

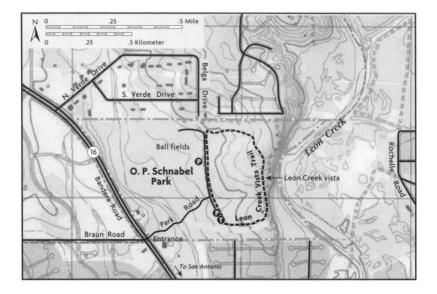

hard to describe a set route in the back part of the park. If you have time and you and your pooch are up for it, you can wander the back part of the park for hours, on everything from narrow, steep trails scrambling down hillsides, to open grassy areas, wide dirt paths through tall trees, and the rocky creekbed with a cliff on one side—in short, a veritable noodle bowl of trails crisscrossing the park, which is hemmed by neighborhoods on two sides and the Alamo Country Club golf course behind (in other words, just walk long enough and you will eventually come to one of these boundaries and can follow it around to the main park area). Just keep eyes and ears open for joggers and mountain bikers.

To follow the Leon Creek Vista Trail, start at the far end of the parking lot, to your right as you face the pavilion, restrooms, and playground. The trail, a surface of rough concrete (much cooler than asphalt), is fairly narrow and winds through tall trees and thick underbrush. You will likely pass joggers and animals such as rabbits, roadrunners, and deer. You can hear and see a wealth of birds and enjoy butterflies and wildflowers pretty much year-round.

The trail rises gradually, alternating shade and sun and passing numerous paths leading into the woods, but resist these unless you just want to wander. The trail follows the edge of a high bluff over Leon Creek at about a half mile, so you may want to walk over and look, but be careful as this is pretty high up. A bit farther is a large picnic pavilion on the left, and

Shade covers much of O. P. Schnabel Park. Unpaved trails are not marked but they beckon adventurous dogs and their owners.

on the right, an overlook with a shady bench—the official Leon Creek Vista and a good place to rest. Continue from here, still going up slightly, through fairly dense vegetation to a somewhat jarring reminder that you are, in fact, in a big city—a transmission tower. The trail then turns left to follow the boundary of the park, and there are houses on the other side, some with barking dogs, so be ready if your dog tends to get excited at that prospect. Flocks of doves bursting up from the undergrowth and the occasional dashing squirrel will keep your dog on his toes, too.

At 0.7 mile, the main trail turns left, away from the houses, although you can continue straight here to the park road. This last stretch has more open space with a lot of sotol plants and, at one point, a dirt trail heads off to the left and will take you back to the parking area. The paved path goes right, and you can stick to it and be back at the parking area in less than an hour either way.

23. Eisenhower Park, Yucca and Hill View Trails

Distance: 2.5-mile loop
Hiking time: 1.5 hours
Difficulty: Moderate
High point: 1300 feet
Elevation gain: 170 feet
Best hiking season: October through May
Regulations: Dogs must be on leash; stay on designated trails
Map: USGS Castle Hills and Camp Bullis 7.5' Quadrangles; *San Antonio Parks and Recreation Eisenhower Park Trail Guide*
Contact: San Antonio Parks, Natural Areas Section, 210-698-1057, *www.sanaturalareas.org*

Getting there: From downtown San Antonio, take Interstate 10 west to Loop 1604 east. Take the exit for NW Military Highway, and turn left. Follow this road 2 miles to the park entrance, on the left just before the gate for Camp Bullis.

Notes: Six primitive campsites; advance reservations required (210-207-PARK). Dog mitts are provided at several points along the route, along with signs reminding you that dog poop that isn't picked up finds its way to the drinking water supply (yuck!). This hike is best in cooler weather or cloudy days, as it is sunny and dry and there is no water on the route, so be sure you carry enough for you and Fido. There are shaded pavilions, restrooms, and water fountains at the parking area.

This rugged urban park offers a number of trail options. The Hill View Trail is the longest, following the perimeter for roughly 2.5 miles. But a significant portion, a wide, rocky, partially shady uphill route going clockwise from the parking area, hews close to a tall fence with a noisy quarry

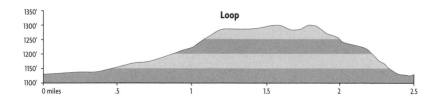

on the other side, then along some very large and noisy powerlines. A better alternative is to head in a clockwise direction on the Yucca Trail, which is paved for about a quarter mile, then becomes a narrow route, alternately smooth dirt and rocky jumble that resembles a streambed more than a trail. It winds in and out of cedar trees and gradually climbs until it joins the Cedar Flats Trail—the trails here are very well marked. Even though this roadlike trail is asphalt surface, it is flanked by lush growth. The shade is patchy, though, and the black surface can get hot, so you may want to pack the dog booties.

Turn left onto the Cedar Flats Trail, which quickly becomes steep, heading up to intersect the Hill View Trail. Even though your route heads right here, take a short detour left to the observation tower and up a short flight of stairs for a view of San Antonio in the distance (and that pesky

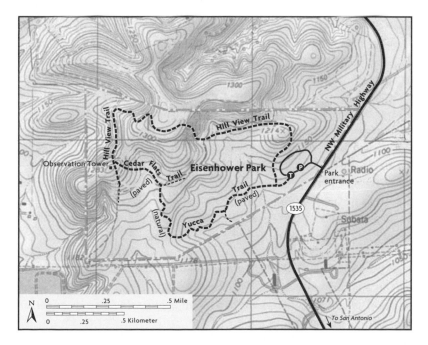

The view from this observation tower at the high point of Eisenhower Park includes the city of San Antonio.

quarry). Then retrace your steps back to the intersection and continue on the Hill View Trail, which now descends sharply and becomes rocky and narrow. There are shady stretches and a breeze in the open expanses. Coming out of some trees and heading up again, you may see a roadrunner dawdling on the trail ahead.

At about 1.5 miles, there is an upward scramble that requires some decent jumps of your dog. Then you head into the shade again, across a smooth, flat area, then up again, then down, and up again—plenty of variety, in other words. You and your dog won't find peace and quiet here—airplanes pass overhead, there is noise from the quarry, and if you think you hear thunder under a clear sky, it is more likely exercises on the adjacent military base—but on weekdays you are likely to find solitude. At about 2 miles, you hit asphalt again, which heads downhill to the parking area.

24. Cibolo Nature Center

Distance: 2.5-mile loop
Hiking time: 1.5 hours
Difficulty: Easy
High point: 1380 feet
Elevation gain: 10 feet
Best hiking season: Year-round
Regulations: Dogs must be on leash
Map: Cibolo Nature Center Meet the Trails
Contact: Cibolo Nature Center, 830-249-4616, *www.cibolo.org*

Getting there: From downtown San Antonio, take Interstate 10 west 30 miles to exit 542, US Highway 87 north. Bear right at the exit and follow Highway 87 into town, then turn right at State Highway 46, also known as River Road, to New Braunfels. About a mile down this road, turn right onto City Park Road and follow it to the entrance to the nature center on the right.

Notes: No entrance fee but donations accepted for park upkeep. There are restrooms and water at the visitors center.

Start at the visitors center at the far end of the parking lot. Inside, you can purchase *A Guide for the Cibolo Wilderness Trail,* which will help you identify plants and other interesting things along the route. There are trails through four types of habitat here—marsh, prairie, creek, and woodlands—and our route passes through all of them. The Woodland Trail begins (or ends, depending on your direction) just north of the building complex and is a narrow, leafy passage into tall trees. Not far along, bear right at a fork and follow the trail along a high bluff over Cibolo Creek. You and your dog will enjoy the shade and interesting tangles of vines among the trees and the leaf-covered, soft trail with plenty to sniff and interesting roots across the trail. The quite-likely presence of poison ivy is an extra incentive to stick to the trails here.

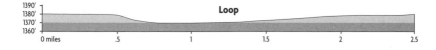

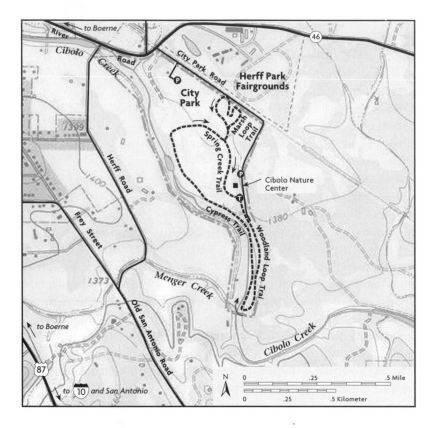

You'll pass two steep stairways that are shortcuts to the creek below, and a bench at an overlook, a nice spot from which to contemplate the creek and soak up the sound of running water. There's another bench at about a half mile where you might want to pause and listen to the crickets and birds. At about three-quarters of a mile, the trail veers right and descends the bluff to the creek and a stretch aptly named The Narrows, which is a scramble over rocks and around towering cypress trees with knobby knees protruding from the clear stream. There are running shallows and quiet, deep pools your dog will enjoy drinking from. But since this is a nature center, he will need to stay on leash. You may want to carry a stick to clear the spiderwebs from this little-used stretch of trail. Look to your right at about a mile for an interesting cliff overhang and, often, vibrating clumps of daddy longlegs spiders. Right after crossing a small bridge over a stream, the landscape opens up; the wide shore at this point has a playground and picnic tables and the creek is shallow

This stretch of the Cibolo Nature Center trail system becomes a tangle of roots from the tall cedars lining Cibolo Creek.

with a flat bank. Skip a few rocks while your pooch gets a drink and cools his feet.

Continue straight ahead on the Cypress Trail, which runs between the towering, green bald cypress trees marking the creek on one side and tall, tall grasses in the meadow on the other. This part is sunny, and frequented by butterflies most of the year. The trail heads away from the creek soon, and then there is a city recreation facility on your left, its tennis courts and parking lot a somewhat unwelcome intrusion on the nature, although it doesn't seem to bother the birds or butterflies. The nature center has planted trees that will eventually buffer hikers from this noise. The trail shortly turns back toward the visitors center area, but take a left on the Marsh Loop, a diversion of about a half mile that is mostly boardwalk over, of course, a marsh. Stay to the right at the fork and look for dragonflies on and fish under the water, perhaps a vulture on top of a cypress—and the occasional loose board.

The trail circles to the left and eventually rejoins where you turned off onto Marsh Loop, which leads to the Spring Creek Trail. Take a short diversion to the left to see a reproduction of dinosaur tracks discovered in the area. Then stay on the Spring Creek Trail, following the creek, until the Shortcut crossing, which will return you to the visitors center.

25. Medina River Park, Rio Medina Trail

Distance: 3 miles round trip
Hiking time: 1.5 hours
Difficulty: Easy
High point: 560 feet
Elevation gain: 60 feet
Best hiking season: Year-round
Regulations: Dogs must be on leash; scoop and pack out waste; stay on designated trails
Map: San Antonio Parks Medina River Park Trails
Contact: San Antonio Parks, Natural Areas Section, 210-698-1057, *www.sanaturalareas.org*

Getting there: From downtown San Antonio, take Interstate 35 south about 15 miles to the State Highway 16 exit to Poteet, and head south

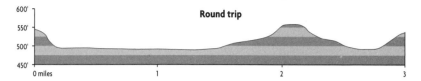

about 4 miles until you see the Medina River bridge. Look for the entrance to Medina River Park on the left side of the divided highway. The official address is 15890 Highway 16 South.

Notes: Camping is by reservation only (210-207-7275). There are restrooms and posted information at the trailhead parking lot.

This 364-acre natural area became a city park in 2005, a joint project of the San Antonio Parks Foundation, the San Antonio Parks and Recreation Department, the Kronkowsky Foundation, and Texas Parks and Wildlife. It includes areas on both sides of the river, with group camping on the south side and, on the north side, a covered pavilion, restrooms, and 2.6 miles of trails that range from 8-foot-wide pavement to narrow dirt paths. There are plans to add more land and more than 10 miles of trails to the park.

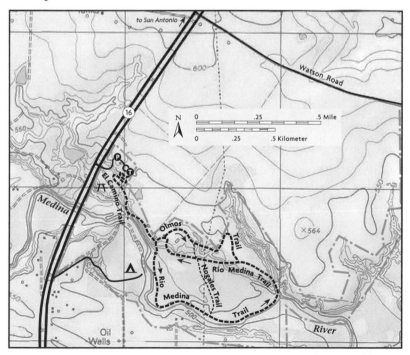

The green Medina River flows swiftly past the wooded banks in Medina River Park.

From the parking area, head down the wide pavement of the El Camino Trail, named after the wagon trail many settlers followed into the area, which switches back through slopes of wildflowers to the picnic pavilion, then down to the junction with the gravel portion of the Rio Medina Trail. Here, you can keep going straight about 50 yards to a river overlook. Due to strong and unpredictable currents, no swimming is allowed, so hold on to your dog. There are other points along the way where thirsty pooches can get a drink, but not here. After that little detour, go back, turn right onto the gravel trail, and head into the trees, accompanied by the sounds of frogs, the breeze through leaves, and birdcalls.

The trail parallels the river, which in spring and summer is mostly obscured by vegetation, although there are numerous splits to the shore. The trail soon rises above the banks. Watch for spiderwebs across this little-used path and for numerous stinkbugs. You don't want your pooch to disturb these cranky critters. At the split, stay to the right and follow the river, which rushes around cedar trunks and over rocky shoals. A short side trail here leads to the water. Now you are on packed dirt, in tall trees with occasional open spaces, and quickly too high above the river to reach the water. There will be lizards scurrying through the leaves that may interest your dog and a lot of varied bird sounds for you. The air is typically still down here in the river cut, which is very woodsy and quiet. Vines entangle the trees, and old barbed wire fences recall days when this was farm and ranch land.

The trail intersects a cross trail, the Nogales Trail, then continues back closer to the water, where low shoals create a place where it is safe for your dog to drink or for you to fill her water bowl. But remember, the current is swift, so no swimming! Dragonflies, butterflies, and all manner of other insects are abundant here. Thick tangles of vines, à la Tarzan, climb big oaks. Turn away from the river at about eight-tenths of a mile; the trail opens up a bit, which means fewer webs. There are many more vines, though, and patches of inland sea oats.

After a slight rise up the riverbank, the trail intersects with the Olmos Trail. At this intersection, you may spy a very large owl, and if you watch the trail, you also might see owl pellets. Stay to the left, on gravel that is fine enough to be easy on the paws, until the second intersection with the Olmos Trail. This time, turn right onto this trail, which goes higher up and leads through more typical south Texas vegetation—cactus, mesquite, and yucca. There is little shade, but still dragonflies and butterflies, and a breeze! For a few hundred yards, you walk next to plowed fields and a view of a cement plant, but then the path veers away so all you can see is the natural vegetation. The Olmos Trail takes you back about a half mile, then reconnects with the Rio Medina Trail at that first intersection (look for the owl again, if you didn't see him the first time). Double back over part of the Rio Medina until you reach where you turned off onto the Olmos Trail, and now continue on to close the main loop at about 1.5 miles. Then head back the way you came in along the river bluff until you hit pavement, and follow it to where you parked.

26. Government Canyon State Natural Area, Lytle's Loop

Distance: 4.8-mile loop
Time: 2.4 hours
Difficulty: Easy to moderate
High point: 1040 feet
Elevation gain: 50 feet
Best hiking season: Spring through fall
Regulations: Dogs are restricted to Frontcountry trails and must be on leash; hikers yield to horses; stay on designated trails; no camping or overnight use
Map: Texas Parks and Wildlife Government Canyon State Natural Area
Contact: Government Canyon State Natural Area, 210-688-9055, *www.tpwd.state.tx.us/spdest/findadest/parks/government_canyon*

Getting there: From Loop 1604 west of San Antonio, take Culebra Road/ Farm to Market Road 471 west (away from town) for 3.5 miles. Turn right onto Galm Road and go 1.6 miles to the park entrance on the left.

Notes: Entrance fee. This is a relatively new park with more than 36 miles of trails in two areas, the Frontcountry and the Backcountry. The park is open Fridays through Mondays only. Gates are open 8:00 AM to 7:00 PM, but access to trails ends at 5:00 PM. Hikers should plan to be off all trails before sunset. The more dramatic scenery is in the Backcountry; if your dog has other plans for the day, check out some of these trails, too. There are guided hikes periodically (check the website for a schedule).

Texas Parks and Wildlife purchased this 8600-plus-acre park in cooperation with a number of other partners, including government, nonprofit and private entities, and individuals. It lies on the Balcones Escarpment, an area of canyons that are the easternmost boundary of the Edwards Plateau, and nearly 90 percent of the land is over the recharge zone for the Edwards

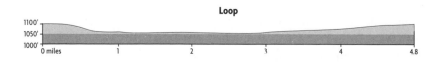

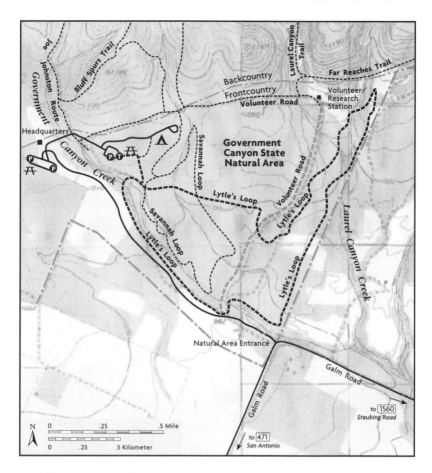

Aquifer, the source of drinking water for San Antonio. There are two trails in the Frontcountry, which is open to dogs: the 2.3-mile Savannah Loop and the 4.8-mile Lytle's Loop. They share a trailhead and parking area with water faucets and portable toilets. The Lytle's Loop trail alternates between woods, thick brush, and open areas, including a savannah restoration area. The surface is mostly dirt with some rocky areas.

From the parking area, head down the trail to a T intersection, and turn right. The trails are well marked, and you will be following numbered markers with a purple symbol for the trail. After you turn, a section of the trail follows a gravel and dirt road that parallels the park entrance road, and you may hear some vehicle noise. After crossing another gravel road, the trail again becomes a dirt track and heads through trees, then down and across Government Canyon Creek, which is usually dry. Soon, you pass the first of several impressive, majestic old oak trees. Mountain laurel, juniper, mesquite, live oak, and buckeye are common throughout the park and in this long, wooded stretch of the hike. These wooded areas are interspersed with open, grassy meadows where you will see wildflowers in season.

The trail twice crosses Laurel Canyon Creek, which is also usually dry. After recrossing the gravel road you came over earlier (it leads to a research station at the back of the Frontcountry), the trail follows an asphalt road for about 5 yards, then turns into a savannah area before winding and twisting through brush and trees. Butterflies are abundant on the trail most of the year, and you will hear the constant chirp of cardinals and whir of wings and the rustling of small wildlife in the brush. Pairs or groups of doves occasionally burst from the grass, too. You are likely to meet other hikers, many with dogs, as well as bike riders and even joggers on this trail.

Little Max, with owner Veronica, enjoys the Frontcountry at Government Canyon State Natural Area.

27. Palmetto State Park

Distance: 2.2 miles round trip
Hiking time: 1 hour
Difficulty: Easy
High point: 310 feet
Elevation gain: 10 feet
Best hiking season: Year-round
Regulations: Dogs must be on leash
Map: Texas Parks and Wildlife Palmetto State Park
Contact: Palmetto State Park, 830-672-3266,
www.tpwd.state.tx.us/parks/palmetto

Getting there: From Interstate 10 east of San Antonio, take US Highway 183 south a couple of miles to Park Road 11, and turn right. Follow the park road 2 miles to the park headquarters, just past the intersection with Farm to Market Road 1586. Continue on Park Road 11, over Oxbow Lake, the San Marcos River, and Rutledge Creek, and turn left to follow it to parking for the day-use area.

Notes: Entrance fee. The park has campsites with water and electricity and water only, a group camping and picnic area, and playgrounds. Pedal boats and canoes can be rented for use on Oxbow Lake, where fishing is also allowed. The San Marcos River is popular for canoeing.

This park along the San Marcos River is an area where the ranges of eastern and western vegetation species merge. It is named for the tropical dwarf palmetto plants that blanket a usually swampy area of the park. These are plants found in east and southeast Texas, but rarely north and west of here. Three trails that start within a short distance of each other can be combined for a hike with a variety of landscapes and scenery. The parking lot is next to the picnic shelter, a converted refectory built by the Civilian Conservation Corps in the 1930s of native rock and, originally, a roof of thatched palmetto.

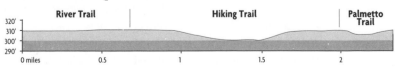

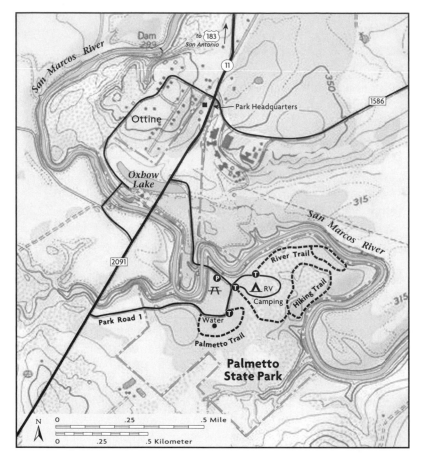

From here, walk down the road along the river toward the RV camping area and the start of the River Trail. This dirt trail, two-thirds of a mile, parallels the river for a distance, through tall trees, brush, and grasses. Debris deposited along this high bank by the river in flood stage provides ample opportunities for your dog to investigate. You will hear the calls of many birds, as this park is a birding hot spot where more than 240 species have been identified, including crested carcaras, prothonotary warblers, and red-shouldered hawks. Listen for the persistent knocking of woodpeckers, too. You and your pooch will also hear plenty of rustling in the brush and are likely to see armadillo rooting in leaves near the trail, mostly unconcerned about your presence.

Follow the sandy trail to where it forks and bear right. You will loop around through trees and back to the river, where there is a short but steep access to the water. The river generally has a strong current, although pups can safely get a drink where it is shallow. Continue around the loop and back out the way you came. Another trail, named simply the Hiking Trail, starts about 15 yards back up the road on your left. Just a few yards in, look on your left for an old metal wheel that trees have grown right through and around. This 1.4-mile trail takes you close to some of the park's namesake plants and past the site of mud boils that have been inactive since the 1970s, then winds among a variety of trees intertwined with vines.

When the trail forks, turn right to drop into a low area of trees with grass beneath. You are likely to see deer in this area and might spot an owl, too. As you round the loop portion, there is a trail leading off to the right to the RV camping area. Continue past that, back up and along the bank until you return to the fork. Turn right and retrace your steps to the beginning of the trail. Turn left at the road and walk down to the Palmetto Trail, a one-third-mile route that circles an ephemeral swamp

Palmetto State Park is named for its abundant stands of dwarf palmetto (Sabal minor), like these around an ephemeral swamp on one of the trails.

The dwarf palmetto plant has distinctive, fan-shaped fronds.

lush with palmettos, then reemerges on the road just a little farther on. Follow the road back to the parking area.

From here, a paved walk goes down and across a low bridge to the campground, if you want a closer look at the San Marcos River. Again, beware of the swift current, and if the water is running over the bridge, do not walk into it.

HILL COUNTRY

28. Pedernales Falls State Park, Wolf Mountain Trail

Distance: 7.4-mile balloon loop
Hiking time: 3.7 hours
Difficulty: Moderate
High point: 1100 feet
Elevation gain: 200 feet
Best hiking season: Year-round
Regulations: Dogs must be on leash
Map: Texas Parks and Wildlife Pedernales Falls State Park
Contact: Pedernales Falls State Park, 830-868-7304,
www.tpwd.state.tx.us/spdest/findadest/parks/pedernales_falls

Getting there: From Austin, take US Highway 290 west 32 miles to Farm to Market Road 3232, turn right and go 7 miles to Farm to Market Road 2766, turn right and then immediately left into the park. From San Antonio, take US Highway 281 to Johnson City, turn right onto Farm to Market Road 2766 and drive 9 miles to the park entrance. Turn right at the first opportunity after the park entrance for the trailhead parking lot.

Notes: Entrance fee. The Pedernales River and low areas are subject to flash floods; do not hike if there has been significant rain or if rain is predicted, and if you notice the water rising, leave the area immediately (visit *www.tpwd.state.tx.us/spdest/findadest/parks/pedernales_falls* for very convincing photographs of the speed and magnitude of these floods).

This hike traverses classic Texas Hill Country terrain, with views of the surrounding area and plenty of variety and a natural spring at the far

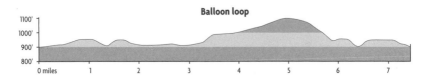

Balloon loop

end of the loop. There are distance markers at every half mile. From the trailhead, the path leads through juniper and oak trees and open spaces, rising up and dipping down for a mile before crossing the usually dry Bee Creek. The surface alternates gravel, rock, and crushed asphalt, with occasional sandy or dirt surfaces. After crossing the creek, you pass through some taller trees—including pecan, elm, sycamore, walnut, and hackberry—mixing shade and sun, then head downhill near 1.5 miles to cross another creek, then pass a primitive camping area. A trail that turns left to the camping area is not on the park trail map; continue straight ahead to the next fork, where there is a sign pointing back to the parking lot.

Stay to the left here, pass the primitive toilets and enter thicker woods and, eventually, cross another creekbed. Just past the 3-mile marker, the trail crosses a meadow, the twin sand ruts almost lost in tall grass and, depending on the season, flowers. Soon you will see a sign for Jones Spring on the left. Take the short detour off the trail, and enjoy the shade and

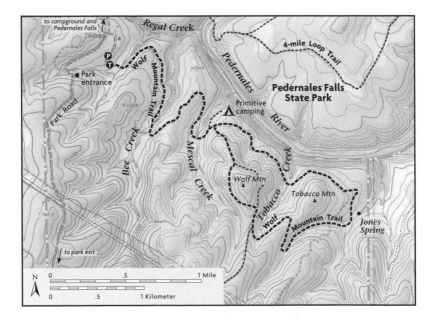

Bridget finds Jones Spring in Pedernales Falls State Park to be a peaceful spot to rest on a long hike.

babble of the flowing spring, which trickles down the rocks into ever-larger pools of water. Look for ferns growing along the edges and, in the water, tadpoles and other tiny creatures. More than 150 species of birds have been seen in this park, and around the spring is a good place to look for some of them. You may also see white-tailed deer, rabbits, armadillos, and other wildlife on the hike.

When you head back to the trail, look for the ruins of an old home-stead just around the corner on your right. Previous visitors have placed shards of pottery and glass from the old dwelling on the rock walls (just remember not to disturb or remove any of these artifacts). The trail passes through openings in the settlement's old stone wall several times. Now the trail narrows and you and your dog will have to negotiate a couple of rocky scrambles. For a mile or so, you are walking on sand and flat rock through tall trees, more or less paralleling a creekbed. Soon a low bluff appears on your right, then the trail turns and climbs the bluff over a bit of scree before leveling off. It then intersects with a wide, level gravel road heading both ways around the peak of Wolf Mountain—you can head either way here—offering views of the surrounding countryside. The trail forms a circle around the peak, so you will reach a T intersection on the other side that heads down toward the primitive campground. There is a sign pointing you back to the parking lot, so you won't get confused and keep circling the mountain (unless you are enjoying the views so much that you just want to). Soon you are back at the trail that brought you in. Turn left and retrace the last 1.8 miles to where you parked.

If you have time, drive to the end of the main park road and take the short hike down to an overlook over Pedernales Falls, one of the most scenic spots in Texas. The river drops 50 feet along a distance of about 3000 feet, flowing over layered limestone that belongs to the 300-million-year-old Marble Falls Formation, part of the southeast edge of the Llano Uplift. From the overlook, you can walk down to the water's edge, but swimming is not allowed in the falls area. This area is subject to flash flooding, too, so do not venture down to the water if it is raining or has recently rained. Check conditions at the park headquarters.

29. Guadalupe River State Park, Loop Trails

Distance: 5.3 miles round trip
Hiking time: 2.75 hours
Difficulty: Moderate
High point: 1200 feet
Elevation gain: 75 feet
Best hiking season: Year-round
Regulations: Dogs must be on leash; stay on designated trails
Map: Texas Parks and Wildlife Guadalupe River State Park
Contact: Guadalupe River State Park, 830-438-2656,
   www.tpwd.state.tx.us/spdest/findadest/parks/guadalupe_river

Getting there: From San Antonio, take US Highway 281 to State Highway 46 and turn left. After 7 miles, turn right onto Park Road 31, which dead-ends into the park. Trailhead parking is at the end of a short gravel road immediately to the right of the park entrance.

Notes: Entrance fee. The trail is shared with bicycle and horseback riders. Gate is locked each evening; those who do not have a camping permit

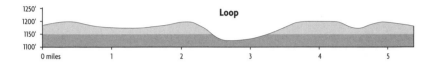

must leave by 10:00 PM. This 1938-acre park has 4 miles of frontage on the Guadalupe River, a cold, clear stream that passes through some of the most scenic country in Texas. Many park visitors enjoy tubing or canoeing the river rapids, as well as swimming, fishing, or just relaxing under the huge bald cypress trees lining the banks. Exercise caution, however, as there can be strong currents and hazards such as rocks in the river. There is easy river access from the day-use area, which has parking, restrooms, and picnic tables. Camping options include a walk-in campground and sites for RVs and tents.

There is a stock tank at the trailhead, as well as benches and a picnic table in the shade. Head down the dirt and rock double track, which gradually

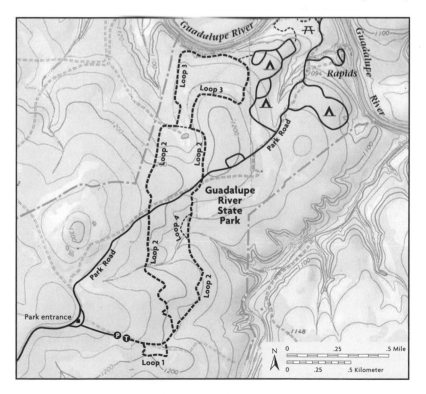

The scenic Guadalupe River winds below the hiking trail in the state park named after the river.

descends, hiking between scattered trees and brush on either side. Soon you will pass a turnoff for Loop 1. You can take it now and come back along the main trail, or stick to the main trail now and hit the loop on your way back. Both alternatives will minimize backtracking. After passing where Loop 1 rejoins the main trail, you will come to another fork, which is the start of Loop 2. The trail is very well marked with indicators showing the direction of the trail and the trail number. Stay to the right on a narrower dirt trail with scattered rock through open and sunny grasslands interspersed with the shade of junipers and oaks. Winding through this Hill Country landscape, your dog will be intrigued by the many scents, and you will hear, and possibly see, numerous birds. Deer and armadillos are common in the park, as are dozens of species of birds, and lucky visitors may also see fox, coyote, and bobcat.

The turnoff for Loop 4, which makes a 0.4-mile half circle and returns to the main trail, is on your left. It is up to you whether to take this little detour. It adds a very small distance to the hike. Either way, continue along Loop 2, which soon crosses the main park road. Signs and speed bumps slow the traffic, but look both ways, as this park can be busy.

You and your dog will pass through more grasslands and encounter a couple of shady benches on the right, then you come to a turnoff to Loop 3. If you continue around on Loop 2 and return to where you started, that will be a hike of 3 miles. Loop 3 is a more rugged, rocky trail that offers views of the beautiful Guadalupe River, so if you are up for the entire 5.3-mile distance, turn right. For a while, the double-track trail is grass and soft dirt, where you will likely see deer tracks. Then the double track veers to the right and the trail goes left, becoming narrow and rocky. Not far beyond this is an intersection with a trail from the campground area of the park; larger dogs will be able to drink from the water trough provided here for horses.

There is more shade on this far side of Loop 3, which is rugged and rocky, tracing the top of a bluff above the Guadalupe River. Several short detours angle over to the edge for those who want to take a look, but be careful, as it is a sharp drop-off and a long way down. The trail veers close to the edge briefly, then turns away from the river. The uneven rocks continue for a while before giving way to grass and dirt once again. You will walk through open grass, then through a nice stand of tall trees and up a rocky slope. Then it is back into the open, on a double track through tall, rippling grass, before crossing back over the park road. You wind through junipers and oaks again, which creak in the wind and throw dappled sunlight on the dirt and scattered rocks of the trail, before meeting up with the intersection where you started Loop 2. Retrace your steps from here, taking Loop 1 for variety if you did not do so on the way out, and return to the parking area.

30. Colorado Bend State Park, Spicewood Springs Trail

Distance: 5.2-mile loop
Time: 2.5 hours
Difficulty: Moderate
High point: 1300 feet
Elevation gain: 270 feet
Best hiking season: Spring through fall
Regulations: Dogs must be on leash and are not allowed in the creek
Map: Texas Parks and Wildlife Colorado Bend State Park
Contact: Colorado Bend State Park, 325-628-3240,
   www.tpwd.state.tx.us/spdest/findadest/parks/colorado_bend

Getting there: Take US Highway 183 north from Austin to Lampasas, then take Farm to Market Road 580 west and drive 24 miles to Bend. Follow signs 4 miles, 2 miles of which are on unpaved road, to the park entrance. Once inside the park, it is 6 miles on unpaved road to park headquarters and parking. From the park headquarters, drive through the walk-in camping area and park at the picnic area near the boat ramp.

Notes: Entrance fee. The park entrance is subject to flooding, so it is advisable to leave the park if heavy rain is expected. All caves are closed except to tours. The park closes some weekdays during hunting season; call ahead or check the calendar of events on the website. There are spigots of potable water and composting toilets near the walk-in camping area.

This park, located on a bend of the picturesque upper Colorado River above Lake Buchanan, has 12.3 miles of hiking trails. While many of those miles are through typical Hill Country landscape, there is also a trail along Spicewood Creek, which cascades for more than a mile down the hillside, and a stretch under tall trees along the river.

The trail starts at the gate at the end of the parking area. For a half mile, it is a dirt and grass road along the flat, grassy bank of the river

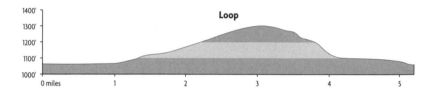

under occasional pecan and cottonwood trees. At a marker, the trail turns right and heads up the slope. Almost immediately you and your dog will cross the creek—look for the trail marker on the other side—the first of many crossings. Thanks to strategically placed stones, the crossings can generally be made with dry feet, but you may want to pack an extra pair of socks just in case. After this first crossing, you are on a narrow, rocky traverse of the hillside 20 feet or so above the water, which is a series of waterfalls and pools. Above a couple more falls, the water level matches that of the trail, and you cross again at a shallow, calm spot. The trail is over rock here, and dogs will have to jump a bit.

Another crossing above a waterfall takes you back to the rocky hillside and then another creek crossing. A narrow stretch of trail leads to the largest of the route's pools, and you may want to stop here for a bit to

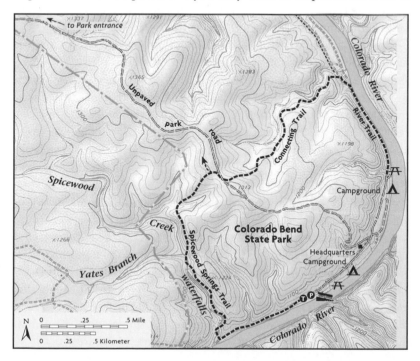

enjoy the scenery and sound of the waterfall. Just remember that the creek is a fragile environment and dogs are not allowed in the water. The trail heads to the right of this pool, along a sloped rock bank where footing may prove tricky for you and your dog (the water below is, fortunately, shallow), then continues up. At the next creek crossing, the stepping-stones can be a little hard to follow, so take your time. The ground on the other side is muddy from several spring seeps. Another crossing of the creek returns you to the other side, where the trail veers away from the creek and into the trees for a ways before returning to cross it yet again. This crossing is a bit tricky, too, requiring you to actually step up a low waterfall. Follow the bank for a short distance before making the final crossing and heading through trees and then along an open stretch of grassy bank.

Then the route takes you to your right away from the creek, heading uphill on a rocky trail through junipers and brush. After a long climb, you reach an intersection, where you will turn right for a short walk to a trailhead parking area. Cross the park road and pick up the trail a short distance down. This 1.2-mile section of the trail is more of a typical Hill Country hike, a winding and rocky dirt trail through cactus and brush. The trail descends steadily, then levels off in taller brush for a while before continuing to descend.

After a bit more winding, you come out into the open and a wide, mowed track through tall grass. At the intersection, turn right again onto the River Trail, which heads down and across a wash, then back up to parallel the riverbank. You will walk about a mile on a wide trail under tall trees with the river below you on your left and a cliff on your right. The trail emerges into a picnic area parking lot. Follow the road about eight-tenths of a mile through the developed part of the park, past a camping area, park headquarters, and the walk-in camping area, back to your car.

At least 155 species of birds have been spotted in the park, including golden-cheeked warblers and bald eagles. Colorado Bend is also popular for fishing, especially during the spring white bass run. In addition to the main camping areas, there are two backpack areas, the River Backpack Area, which you passed on this hike, and the Windmill Backpack Area on the Upper Gorman Creek Trail. The park is also known for Gorman Falls, a 60-foot-high falls with travertine formations and lush vegetation. The falls can be viewed only on guided tours (check the calendar of events), and dogs are not allowed due to the fragile nature of the area.

The trail in Colorado Bend State Park follows Spicewood Creek, which tumbles over a number of travertine falls on its way to the Colorado River.

31. Enchanted Rock State Natural Area, Loop Trail

Distance: 4.5-mile loop
Time: 2.5 hours
Difficulty: Easy to moderate
High point: 1600 feet
Elevation gain: 160 feet
Best hiking season: Spring through fall
Regulations: Dogs must be on leash and are not allowed to swim in any water (but let them drink to their hearts' content); scoop and pack out waste
Map: Texas Parks and Wildlife Enchanted Rock State Natural Area
Contact: Enchanted Rock State Natural Area, 325-247-3903, *www.tpwd.state.tx.us/spdest/findadest/parks/enchanted_rock*

Getting there: From Austin, take State Highway 290 west 78 miles to Fredericksburg, where the highway becomes Main Street. From San Antonio, take Interstate 10 west to US Highway 87 north and continue 70 miles to Fredericksburg; turn left onto Main Street. From Fredericksburg, turn right onto Ranch Road 965, which arrives at Enchanted Rock State Natural Area in 17 miles.

Notes: This is one of the most popular parks in Texas, and when it reaches capacity no one else is allowed in. Avoid this problem by arriving early (best in hot summer anyway) or by coming midweek. Improved campground and three primitive areas are available by reservation. There are also picnic areas.

Enchanted Rock is one of the nation's largest batholiths—an underground rock formation uncovered by erosion—a 640-acre dome of pink granite rising 425 feet above the surrounding countryside. Tonkawa Indian legend and mystery surround the formation, designated a National Natural

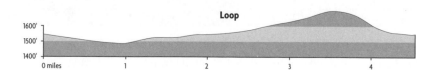

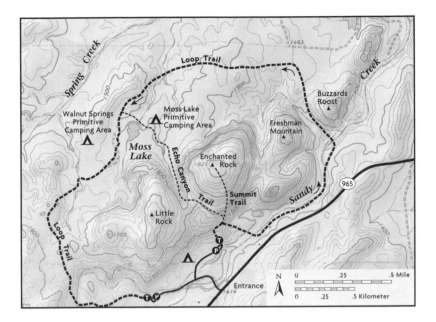

Landmark in 1970 and opened as a state park in 1984. From the Loop Trail, hikers can view all sides of Enchanted Rock and its environs.

The trail is, of course, a loop, but a tiny segment of it is on park road, so leave your car near your finish point—to the left of the park entrance past the playground—and get that out of the way early. Follow the road past camping areas to the parking lot at the opposite end. There are two options here, head left to cross the creek immediately and start the loop, or turn right for a stretch of the Summit Trail. This option will give you a closer look at the park namesake; there is even a telescope that affords a peek at the top. Then bear right to cross Sandy Creek, which may require getting feet and paws wet, depending on the time of year and recent rains, and head toward the unpoetically but aptly named Buzzards Roost.

Following the creek, the trail here is narrow and, in parts, shady. You may encounter red slider turtles and will certainly be hearing and seeing a variety of birds all along the way. Just past a trail that leads to a primitive camping area, cross the creek again—last chance for your dog to get a drink for a while—and pass between Buzzards Roost and Freshman Mountain. The trail surface is mostly crushed granite, but at one spot, what looks like golf-ball–sized hail scattered on the ground is actually an outcropping of white quartz (you can see veins of it occasionally in the granite). You and your pooch will also be crossing exposed granite,

Trees and other vegetation seem to grow right out of the granite at Enchanted Rock State Natural Area.

which can get quite hot in the sunshine. Bring dog booties if you have them, and think about getting some if you don't.

After a bit of an uphill stretch, you will be behind Enchanted Rock, on a wide road. This part is soft and easier on the paws. There are frequent fabulous views of the rock, and if you look closely you may see people climbing it. There are fewer trees here but riotous wildflowers from spring through fall. Coyote scat is a frequent sight on the trail, deer graze brazenly in midday, and you may see an occasional snake. Look for small striped frogs in the water crossings. There is a turnoff for the Moss Lake Primitive Camping Area, and a compost toilet is located near this intersection. A little farther is another turnoff for Moss Lake, which is worth a detour unless you are planning to hike the Echo Canyon Trail (Hike 32), which will take you right past the lake.

The next two turnoffs make a loop around the Walnut Springs Primitive Camping Area. In the fourth mile, there is a tangle of large boulders, including some intriguing cavelike cracks, for you and your dog to explore. You can catch good views of the surrounding Hill Country from this high point, too. Then you head downhill, over rock and around cactus, to the parking area. If you parked here, you're done. If you parked at the other end of the paved area, you have about a quarter mile still to go. Follow the parking area past restrooms on your right and campsites on your left back to the Summit Trail parking area.

You may not be able to resist climbing the rock at this point. It is a 425-foot rise in about six-tenths of a mile over rough granite (think dog booties), with a stiff breeze and incredible view waiting at the top.

32. Enchanted Rock State Natural Area, Echo Canyon Trail

Distance: 2 miles round trip
Hiking time: 2 hours
Difficulty: Moderate
High point: 1600 feet
Elevation gain: 100 feet
Best hiking season: Spring through fall
Regulations: Dogs must be on leash and are not allowed to swim in any water; scoop and pack out waste
Map: Texas Parks and Wildlife Enchanted Rock State Natural Area
Contact: Enchanted Rock State Natural Area, 325-247-3903, *www.tpwd.state.tx.us/spdest/findadest/parks/enchanted_rock*

Getting there: From Austin, take State Highway 290 west 78 miles to Fredericksburg, where the highway becomes Main Street. From San

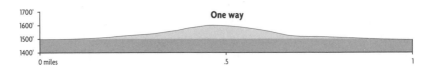

One way

1700'	
1600'	
1500'	
1400'	
0 miles	.5	1

Antonio, take Interstate 10 west to US Highway 87 north and continue 70 miles to Fredericksburg; turn left onto Main Street. From Fredericksburg, turn right onto Ranch Road 965, which arrives at Enchanted Rock State Natural Area in 17 miles. From the park entrance, cross the creek, turn right, and park at the far end, at the Summit trailhead.

Notes: This is one of the most popular parks in Texas and closes when it reaches capacity. Avoid this problem by arriving early (best in hot summer anyway) or coming midweek. Improved campground and three primitive areas are available by reservation. There are also picnic areas.

Echo Canyon Trail passes between Enchanted Rock and Little Rock, and a good third of it is scrambling over and around an amazing jumble of rocks and large boulders. Dogs need to be big and agile enough to do this. If yours is not, consider hiking in the back way from the Loop Trail (Hike 31), which this one intersects, past the lake and into the canyon, turning back and retracing your steps when you reach this rocky part, because this trail offers some stunning and unique sights. Otherwise, take

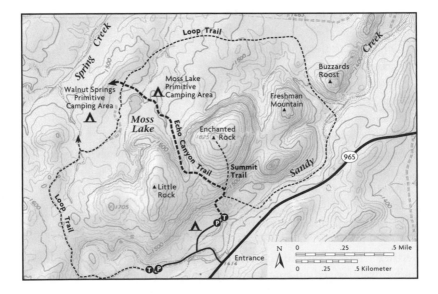

Hikes at Enchanted Rock State Natural Area often involve climbing over and around granite rocks.

Summit Trail from the parking area up Enchanted Rock until you see the Echo Canyon Trail sign off to the left (it will feel like you have climbed most of the way up, but that is hardly the case).

A short way along this trail, you reach the canyon. With giant granite outcroppings rising on either side of you and the rock-strewn gully ahead, you and your dog may think you are on another planet. At the bottom of this scramble is a wide, flat area of tall trees and giant rocks, a good place to rest and catch your breath. The trail follows an intermittent stream from here out into the open behind Enchanted Rock and to Moss Lake. The banks of this half-acre human-made body of water are lush with flowers, cactus, and other plants, and huge trees on the far side. Feel free to hang out a while here, too, just soaking up the serenity of the lake against the dramatic backdrop of Enchanted Rock.

The Echo Canyon Trail crosses the Loop Trail and continues to the Walnut Springs Primitive Camping Area. When you reach the Loop Trail, you can head back the way you came, for a different perspective on the canyon, or take the Loop Trail back. You are just past its midpoint, so turn left for the shortest way around. If you take that way out, when you reach the pavement, follow the road from there back to your car at the Summit Trail parking area.

33. Hill Country State Natural Area, Loop to Wilderness Camp

Distance: 5.8 miles round trip
Hiking time: 3.5 hours
Difficulty: Difficult
High point: 1760 feet
Elevation change: 450 feet
Best hiking season: Year-round
Regulations: Dogs must be on leash; hikers yield to horses, bikers yield to hikers and horses
Map: Texas Parks and Wildlife Hill Country State Natural Area
Contact: Hill Country State Natural Area, 830-796-4413,
  www.tpwd.state.tx.us/spdest/findadest/parks/hill_country

Getting there: From San Antonio, take State Highway 16 northwest to Bandera, then take State Highway 173 south, across the Medina River to State Highway 1077. Turn right and drive 10 miles to where the pavement ends and the road becomes caliche. From here, follow signs to the park headquarters area, where you'll need to obtain a permit (there is a self-pay box if the office is closed). Continue to the trailhead parking, which is at the entrance to the Equestrian Camp at the trailhead.

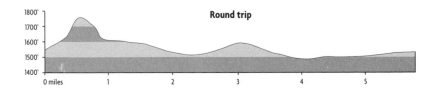

Notes: Entrance fee. There are seven primitive tent campgrounds in the park, as well as equestrian campgrounds, and three designated swimming areas on West Verde Creek, and fishing is allowed as well. There is no drinking water available in the park, except spring water for horses and dogs. Some trails close in wet conditions. The park's website warns, "If you think you need it, we don't got it, you'll need to bring it!" Open weekends only in December and January, all week the rest of the year.

This 5369-acre park, most of it donated by the Merrick Bar-O Ranch with the stipulation that it be kept natural and untouched, has 40 miles of multi-use trails. This particular hike is a classic Hill Country route, traversing rocky hills, canyons, grasslands, oak groves, and creek bottoms, with a side trip to a scenic view that is ample reward for the climbing required.

You can catch Trail 6 between campsites 214 and 215, or just down the road from the parking. You immediately start climbing, and this first half mile offers excellent views of the area, including an 1800s ranch house, fields, and surrounding hills. The trail is sand and loose rock and fairly narrow; if you encounter horseback riders, you will likely have to

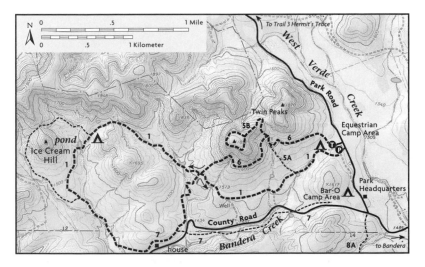

Sotol plants line part of the trail in Hill Country State Natural Area.

step off the trail to let them pass. After a half mile, there is a steep trail to your right, Trail 5B, that leads to the top and around Twin Peaks. This is a worthwhile detour of 0.6 mile round trip—at the top you get a stunning 360-degree panorama—but only if your dog can handle steep, very loose rocky scrambles. Take your time enjoying this view as you circle the top, then return to where you detoured and follow markers to the right for Trail 6, which here skirts the hillside through thick patches of sotol. The saw-toothed leaves draped over the trail can scratch human ankles and dog noses, but before long the sotol thins out and you are on a dirt track through a grassy area with occasional shade from junipers. Look for small blue berries on these trees in the fall.

The trail now goes from being mostly open to surrounded by short trees, flowers, and brush. At the intersection with Trail 1, turn right and follow this mostly level double track through more open country, with gentle rises and falls, into a length of taller trees. There will be butterflies, grasshoppers, and the occasional dung beetle taking advantage of the abundant signs of horses on these trails, and on the entire route plenty of interesting scents for your dog. As you head up and over a small ridge, Trail 1B heads off to the right. If you are feeling particularly energetic and adventuresome, take this steep and rough 1.4-mile circle around Ice Cream Hill. Trail 1B rejoins Trail 1 about a half mile farther along (this loop is not included in the hike distance). Or continue past the Wilderness Camp Area on your left before traversing an open area and skirting a pond. There is access to the water and a nice view of the pond from the far side.

From here, there is an open stretch of about a half mile, then an area of thick trees and brush and a long levee followed by a winding, twisting portion with short up and down scrambles before the trail emerges on a gravel park road. A residence across the road has several vigilant, barking dogs inside a fenced yard, but the trail turns sharply left away from the road and up a steep, narrow scramble into woods. You hike through this wooded area for a while, twisting through some openings in old barbed wire fences, before the trail forks, with Trail 7 to the right and Trail 6A, which you will take, to the left. Just past this intersection is a rough, rocky scramble down, then the trail dead-ends into Trail 6. Turn right for another downward scramble, then a pleasant, shady stretch, followed by several more scrambles before intersecting with Trail 1. Take it to the right and head into the open pretty much for the rest of the hike.

As you pass through open meadows, look for deer or just watch the

The pond just past Wilderness Camp in Hill Country State Natural Area is about the halfway point on this hike.

grass rippling in the breeze that is usually blowing. After a half mile, there is a T intersection on the left with Trail 5A, which cuts across to Twin Peaks. Keep going straight, past some thick woods on the left, back to the equestrian camp and trailhead parking.

34. Hill Country State Natural Area, Comanche Bluff Trail

Distance: 4.2 miles balloon loop
Hiking time: 2.5 hours
Difficulty: Moderate
High point: 1600 feet
Elevation change: 150 feet
Best hiking season: Year-round
Regulations: Hikers yield to horses, bikers yield to hikers and horses; dogs must be on leash
Map: Texas Parks and Wildlife Hill Country State Natural Area
Contact: Hill Country State Natural Area, 830-796-4413, *www.tpwd.state.tx.us/spdest/findadest/parks/hill_country*

Getting there: From San Antonio, take State Highway 16 northwest to Bandera, then take State Highway 173 south, across the Medina River to

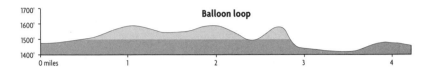

State Highway 1077. Turn right and drive 10 miles to where the pavement ends and the road becomes caliche. From here follow signs to the headquarters area.

Notes: Entrance fee. There are seven primitive tent campgrounds in the park, as well as equestrian campgrounds, and three designated swimming areas on West Verde Creek, and fishing is allowed as well. There is no drinking water available in the park, except spring water for horses and dogs. Some trails close in wet conditions. The park's website warns, "If you think you need it, we don't got it, you'll need to bring it!" Open weekends only in December and January, all week the rest of the year.

This park opened in 1984 and has 40 miles of multiuse trails crisscrossing 5369 acres of grassy valleys, steep limestone hills, and spring-fed

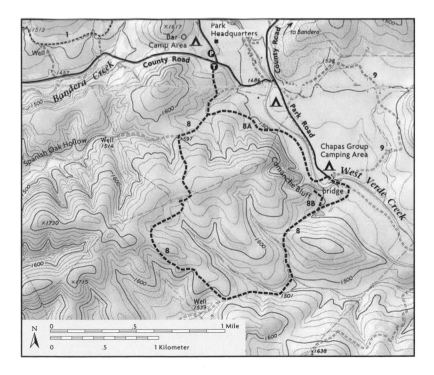

A light rain in Hill Country State Natural Area leaves tiny jewels on vegetation along the trail.

streams. The donors of the bulk of the park's acreage requested that it be kept natural and untouched, so only basic facilities are provided (hence the caveat on the park website). This hike wanders through typical Hill Country landscapes, including rocky slopes, old ranch facilities, and a clear, flowing stream.

From the headquarters area, look for the marker for Trail 8 directly across the road that brought you in. The rock and dirt trail undulates up and down a gentle rise, gradually becoming rockier. You will likely hear the chirps of cardinals and the whirring of their wings, and may glimpse the bright red birds against the green of junipers. Pass the intersection with Trail 8A, which you will be returning on, and continue through the mostly open, grassy area, still going upward. The route follows a barbed wire fence for a while, then goes through an opening to pass an old metal barn and corral on your left before heading down a short slope. At the bottom, on the right, is an amazing patch of several types of cactus.

You will go up and then down again, then turn to follow an electric line, threading up and down a bit more steeply before veering away from the line onto a more narrow dirt and rock track. There is a water tank and old trough at the base of a long hill, and the trail continues heading up and down, winding through several fences. Just after the second fence, look for the marker for Trail 8B on your left. This is a short jaunt with just a bit of scramble to the edge of Comanche Bluff, overlooking West Verde Creek. It is a pretty view, and you can see where you will be on the creekside soon. Rogue trails lead to the left and right, but resist these and backtrack to the main trail, continuing to your left.

The route follows caliche road a short way and crosses the creek. From here, you can see the bluff you were on top of just a few moments earlier. There is a parking area on your left, and the buildings on the right side of the road belong to the Chapas Group Camping Area, which holds twenty campers and has a barn with stalls for nine horses. You can cross the road and take Trail 9, a loop of about 2 miles that will rejoin this one about a half mile from here. But if you go through the parking area and catch Trail 8A at the back of it, you will enjoy some of the prettiest scenery in the park as 8A passes a swimming hole, crosses the creek, then follows along its banks. For about four-tenths of a mile, 8A passes under tall trees and along the creek past campsites, to where the other end of Trail 9 comes in from across the creek. Continue uphill a bit until you meet back up with Trail 8, and retrace your steps to the headquarters area.

35. Lost Maples State Natural Area, East Trail

Distance: 4.6-mile loop
Hiking time: 2 hours
Difficulty: Difficult
High point: 2200 feet
Elevation gain: 400 feet
Best hiking season: Spring and fall
Regulations: Dogs must be on leash; stay on designated trails
Map: Texas Parks and Wildlife Lost Maples State Natural Area
Contact: Lost Maples State Natural Area, 830-966-3413, 800-792-1112, *www.tpwd.state.tx.us/spdest/findadest/parks/lost_maples*

Getting there: From San Antonio, take State Highway 16 northwest 52 miles to Medina, then take Ranch Road 337 west to Vanderpool (this is one of the most scenic drives in the state). The park is 5 miles north of Vanderpool on Ranch Road 187. After obtaining a permit, drive past the campground, and turn right just before crossing the river to the day-use parking area, which has restrooms and picnic tables.

Notes: Entrance fee. Flash floods are common. In case of heavy rain, move to higher ground and do not cross creeks. Don't even think about removing maple leaves from the park. There are forty hike-in primitive campsites (pets allowed on leash) and thirty water and electricity sites.

Beginning at the far end of the parking area, the gravel East Trail follows the Sabinal River along a canyon formed by steep, tree-covered hillsides. You will cross the creek several times, but stepping-stones will keep your feet dry unless there have been recent rains.

This mostly level section of hike can be crowded in the fall months when the leaves take on autumn colors—a relatively rare phenomenon

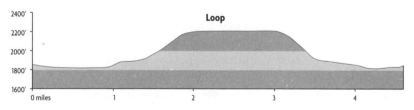

Colorful maples and clear streams on the first part of the hike at Lost Maples State Natural Area.

in most of Texas that occurs here thanks to the park's large, isolated stand of uncommon Uvalde bigtooth maples. Rare birds, such as the colorful green kingfisher, also call the park home. When you pass where Lane Creek flows into the clear Sabinal, it is easy to understand why humans have used this area since prehistoric times, including Spanish explorers, who attempted to colonize the area in the seventeenth century, and Apache, Lipan Apache, and Comanche tribes, who ranged over the area into the nineteenth century. These days, approximately 200,000 people visit this 2174-acre park each year, many of them in the fall, to enjoy the beautiful scenery and vibrant russet colors.

The trail crosses the river again here, then another creek, then heads slightly uphill near a primitive campground, where there is a composting toilet. Continuing, the route hugs the steep banks of a creek for a short stretch (don't cross here) and quickly becomes much more challenging. This is where you will leave the crowds (and the water) behind! There is a long, steep climb of loose limestone and steps, a lot of scrambling, and even some jumps of several feet. A bit more than halfway up is a shady bench where you can rest before continuing up the bluff. Once you and your dog reach the top, the environment is completely different than it was in the canyon. You are now hiking on an open, windswept, and

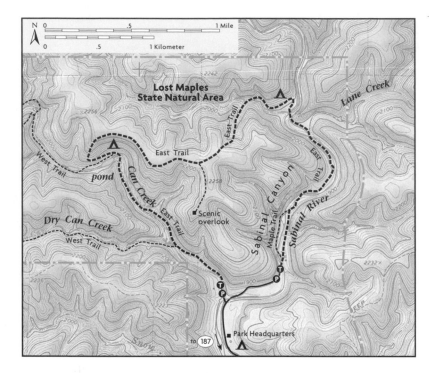

rocky plateau populated by juniper and cactus. Watch for signs of gray fox, deer, armadillo, raccoon, and even javelina and bobcat, both here and in the canyons.

When you reach a T intersection, you can turn right and hike about six-tenths of a mile (round trip) to a scenic overlook, or turn left and continue on the loop. You will have plenty of scenic views from the trail as it follows the edge of the ridge, so the detour isn't really necessary. Take in the view of the west canyon and Can Creek below, which is where you will be shortly. To get there requires a reverse of your climb to the top—a steep, rocky scramble curving around the edge of the bluff. At the bottom, you'll be rewarded by shady trees, a peaceful swimming and fishing hole, and a narrow waterfall. There is another primitive camping area and composting toilet here, and the West Trail, a 4.9-mile route with a 2.5-mile loop at the far side, heads off to your right.

Continue on the East Trail by heading to the left, around the pond. The now-level trail will cross the creek several times before reaching a parking area. Cross this and follow the sign indicating the shortcut to the day-use area to the left to return to where you parked.

The first part of East Trail follows the Sabinal River, across from Maple Trail.

36. South Llano River State Park, Fawn Trail

Distance: 3-mile loop
Hiking time: 1.75 hours
Difficulty: Moderate
High point: 1968 feet
Elevation gain: 188 feet
Best hiking season: Spring through fall
Regulations: Dogs must be on leash
Map: Texas Parks and Wildlife South Llano River State Park
Contact: South Llano River State Park, 325-446-3994,
   www.tpwd.state.tx.us/spdest/findadest/parks/south_llano_river

Getting there: Take Interstate 10 west from San Antonio 114 miles to Junction, and then follow US Highway 377 south through town and then another 5 miles to the park entrance. Follow Park Road 73 to a right turn just before park headquarters. Trailhead parking is on your right.

Notes: Entrance fee. Part of this trail is in a wildlife management area that is closed to the public on many fall and spring weekends. Check with the park for exact dates. There are additional trails in the park's river bottom area, which is closed October 1 through April 1 for roosting turkeys. Gate closed during flooding conditions. RV and tent camping available. Restrooms are located at park headquarters, and there is a water faucet at trailhead parking. There are a parking lot and swimming area where the park road crosses the South Llano River; while dogs aren't allowed in swimming areas, you can walk upstream along the bank a bit and let yours get a drink and cool off.

People have inhabited this part of Texas for 8000 years; the first Anglo settlers arrived in the 1870s. The park itself was formerly a ranch created

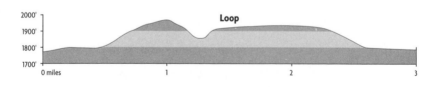

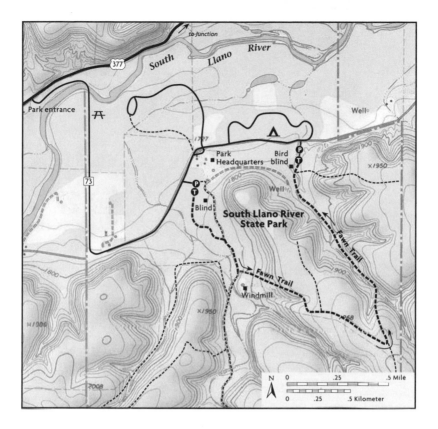

by the Thomas and Buck families, most recently a 2500-plus-acre cattle operation run by Walter Buck Jr., who donated the land to the parks department. Most of the trails are former ranch or maintenance roads, more functional than attractive, and there are still ranch structures, windmills, and stock tanks scattered about the park.

Along the first part of the Fawn Trail, small interpretive signs provide information about many of the native plants, such as blue berry juniper, horse-crippler cactus (which would set a dog back, too), and agarita. Take a look at these while your dog sniffs about. There is a bird blind just off the trail not far from its beginning, where you might see turkeys, cardinals, and vireos if your pooch can sit quietly enough. You will hear a lot of birdcalls on your hike, too.

The crushed granite surface becomes natural dirt, then spills onto a graded dirt and rock road before it forks at a windmill; take the left fork, which heads over a cattle guard and uphill. As you follow the rocky twin

Interpretive signs identify many of the native plants along the first part of the Fawn Trail.

ruts of the trail and climb higher, trees become fewer and good views of the Hill Country are available. At the top of the hill, the route turns left and levels off for a while. Then it heads steeply downhill toward a streambed where a cliff rises on the right and taller trees provide more shade. The trail crosses this rocky streambed a number of times, the surface alternating dirt and rocks, including numerous pieces of flint, which was no doubt useful to the native inhabitants centuries ago. Watch and listen for deer in the brush and lizards dashing out of sight. There will be plenty of scents and sounds to keep your dog interested. Near the end, the trail becomes a wide gravel road, and the last stream crossing is paved, then it dead-ends into another road.

Turn right, then right again at the next road, which leads out to the parking area for walk-in camping. From here, follow the park road through the RV camping area back to park headquarters and the trailhead parking. Or, plan ahead and leave a car here for a 2.6-mile hike. There is another bird blind off to the left just before you reach the walk-in parking area that is worth a visit. The blinds are equipped with photos identifying birds that you might see and windows that open for picture taking.

Sunshine and solitude are plentiful at South Llano River.

37. South Llano River State Park, Wildlife Management Area Trail

Distance: 6.7-mile balloon loop
Hiking time: 3.5 hours
Difficulty: Moderate
High point: 2000 feet
Elevation gain: 220 feet
Best hiking season: Spring through fall
Regulations: Dogs must be on leash
Map: Texas Parks and Wildlife South Llano River State Park
Contact: South Llano River State Park, 325-446-3994,
    www.tpwd.state.tx.us/spdest/findadest/parks/south_llano_river

Getting there: Take Interstate 10 west from San Antonio 114 miles to Junction, and then follow US Highway 377 south through town and then another 5 miles to the park entrance. Follow Park Road 73 to a right turn just before park headquarters. Trailhead parking is on your right.

  Notes: Entrance fee. Part of this trail is in a wildlife management area that is closed to the public on many fall and spring weekends. Check with the park for exact dates. There are additional trails in the park's river bottom area, which is closed October 1 through April 1 for roosting turkeys. Gate closed during flooding conditions. RV and tent camping available. Restrooms are located at park headquarters, and there is a water faucet at trailhead parking. There is a parking lot and swimming area where the park road crosses the South Llano River; while dogs aren't allowed in swimming areas, you can walk upstream along the bank a bit and let yours get a drink and cool off.

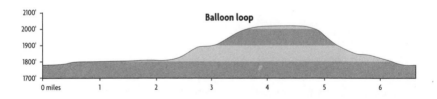

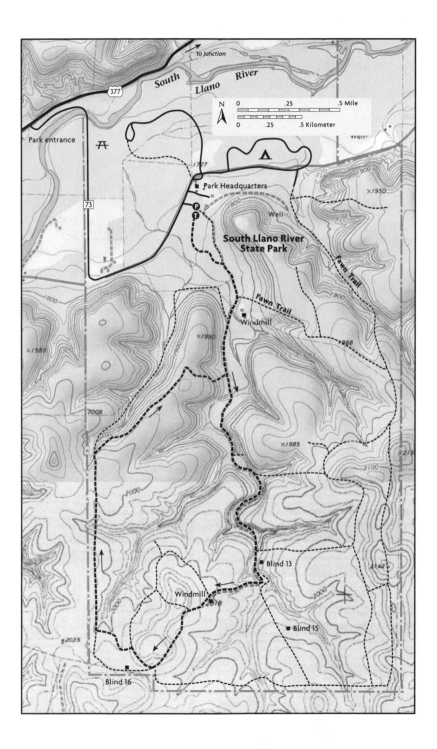

Gravel and dirt roads now used for hike and bike trails (and to provide access to hunting blinds) crisscross the 2155-acre South Llano River State Park Wildlife Management Area. This western edge of the Texas Hill Country is rolling limestone hills covered with dense stands of juniper, live oak, and Spanish oak, and populated by white-tailed deer, jackrabbit, fox, bobcat, and armadillo (look for a confused armadillo frequently rooting around in broad daylight in the grassy yard of the headquarters building).

The first 0.7 mile of this route follows Fawn Trail (Hike 36). The crushed granite and dirt surface is level, with numerous game trails, signs of rooting, and even animal holes for your pup to sniff. Watch for lines of ants heading back and forth from their holes in the ground and busy dung beetles cleaning up after coyotes and other animals. At about a half mile, the trail turns onto a graded road, which soon forks. Stay to the right: a rutted, gently climbing road with trees on either side and an electric fence running alongside the left (usually off, but stay clear anyway). The road can be uneven in places, with patches of loose rock, then it levels off a bit and is softer. On the right are several burned trees, perhaps the result of a lightning strike. Just after you cross a rocky streambed, there is a primitive toilet up steps to the right (your last chance to use any kind of official facilities on the trail).

Continuing, there are several more crossings of the streambed, which at one point has cut a cliff in the limestone. This cliff rising above you and a generous stand of trees create a shady little valley that in the fall and early winter is populated with dozens of migrating monarch butterflies. You will pass two turnoffs to the left (with signs indicating wildlife blinds 10 and 13), then the road veers to the right while a trail continues straight ahead to blind number 15. Follow the road to the right and uphill into more open country and, near the top, a windmill diligently filling an old stock tank. There is a water trough nearby where your dog can get a drink. At the next fork, stay to the left and enjoy the panorama of Hill Country around you, but watch your step on the rock and gravel surface. There is yet another fork, then the trail splits again at a corner of the Wildlife Management Area boundary fence. Stay to the right at this Y, then turn right at the next fork onto a grassy stretch of open road, then left at the next intersection, toward wildlife blind number 16.

With the exception of that last turn, each of the forks after the one at the boundary fence all end up at the same place, another fence marking the western boundary of the park. You reach it in 0.2 mile, and the trail follows it for about 2 miles. But you can turn right, away from the fence,

Collin, Keeper, and Corey pause to look for Monarch butterflies on a shaded stretch of the hike through South Llano River State Park's WMA.

after about eight-tenths of a mile, into a mostly open area scattered with rock and flint. Occasional clumps of cedars offer shade for your dog in hot weather. The trail then heads down a steep hill to intersect with the road you came in on. Retrace your steps from here back to the Fawn Trail and out to the trailhead parking lot.

38. Lake Brownwood State Park, Texas Oak Trail

Distance: 2.25 miles round trip
Hiking time: 1.5 hours
Difficulty: Moderate
High point: 1500 feet
Elevation gain: 50 feet
Best hiking season: Year-round
Regulations: Dogs must be on leash
Map: Texas Parks and Wildlife Lake Brownwood State Park
Contact: Lake Brownwood State Park, 325-784-5223,
   www.tpwd.state.tx.us/spdest/findadest/parks/lake_brownwood

Getting there: From Brownwood, take State Highway 279 north approximately 15 miles and turn right onto Park Road 15. It is about 7 miles to the park entrance. Take the first left turn after the park entrance, toward the Council Bluffs camping area, then another left into the parking area for the trailhead.

   Notes: Entrance fee. Campsites, screened shelter, cabins, and group lodges available by reservation. The park also has picnic areas, boat ramps, swimming areas, and a fishing pier.

At the park entrance, pick up a map and a *Texas Oak Trail* booklet, which corresponds to numbered markers on the first part of the trail. The beginning of the trail is mowed grass surface with mesquite and prickly pear on either side. You cross a maintenance road and a water treatment facility on the left, then the trail veers a bit and the lake is visible through the trees. The sound of boats is common, but so are the calls of cardinals and other birds, as well as the rustling of lizards and squirrels in the grass and trees. The trail becomes mixed gravel and grass and passes several turnoffs for a short handicapped-accessible loop, then narrows and becomes a bit

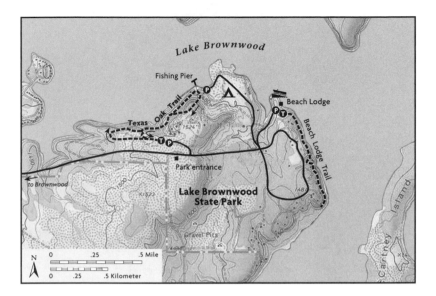

more rugged, following a bluff line above the shore. Continue straight ahead until the trail bears right, down a rocky slope to the water. This is a good place to let your dog get a drink.

The now-narrow and rough trail follows the shore, winding through trees and limestone boulders, many of them covered with a variety of cactus. Depending on the time of year and rain, this stretch can be a bit overgrown, but the trail is still easy to follow, shady, and scenic. Wooden bollards with numbers carved on top help you identify cedar elm, Mexican buckeye, pallid yucca, lace cactus, hawthorn, hackberry, and other plants, using the booklet you picked up at park headquarters.

On this shore-side part of the loop, some of the bollards may be hidden in the brush. Number 16 is easily visible, though, and also marks a turnoff to close the loop, or you can continue farther along the lakeshore. Take the second option if you have time; the path traverses rugged brushy hillsides, open areas abloom with wildflowers in season, a deep wash with fallen trees, and scenic views of the lake. At several points, there is easy access to the water for a drink or to look for turtles sunning themselves on logs. There will be plenty of interesting scents for your dog to sniff all along this route, but stay on the trail and watch for small cactus hidden in the grass.

When the trail hits the parking area for the fishing pier, turn right and follow the pavement a short distance to the return part of the trail.

This forms an almost complete loop, then you retrace your steps a short ways before reaching the fork at marker 16. Head to what is now your left, up a rocky slope and stone steps. Bear left at the top (there is what appears to be a trail to the right, but ignore it) and before long you will be back on the wide, grassy trail near where you started. As you retrace your steps to the parking area, be sure to look up as you pass telephone poles; there is likely to be a buzzard on top of one of them.

If you and your dog want more, drive farther into the park, follow signs to Beach Lodge, and park your car. Another trail follows the lakeshore from Beach Lodge and boat ramp area to the park's screened shelters, about a mile one way. The terrain is slightly different here, and the hike also takes you past a number of stone benches and fire pits, as well as a dramatic stairway leading to the water from the Group Recreation Hall—all constructed of native rock by the Civilian Conservation Corps in the 1930s. Pick up the trail in front of Beach Lodge and follow it along the water to the first group of benches on a point overlooking the lake. The Group Recreation Hall steps are next, then several seating areas after that. The trail is mostly dirt and some rock and shady. There are several confusing forks; for the most part the trail follows the shore, but above it somewhat, and you can always look ahead for the next stone structures. The trail also follows an underground waterline, and the manholes along this are good markers as well. At one fork, you'll see an old pump house on the water to your left, but follow the trail up and to the right. As you approach the cabin area, bear slightly right rather than straight ahead into a gully. Cross the gully on the stone wall, stay to the left of the cabin in front of you, and then pass just below another cabin.

The trail widens out shortly after this, and there are numerous unofficial turnoffs toward the water, which is down a steep slope. Remain on the main trail until just after it rounds a bend in the shore, then follow steps to your left that lead down to a circle drive at the end of a row of screened shelters. Let your dog get a drink in the lake, then turn around and retrace your steps, or plan ahead and leave a car here.

A variety of cacti grow on and around the rocks at Lake Brownwood State Park.

GULF COAST

39. Memorial Park, Purple Trail

Distance: 2.5-mile loop
Hiking time: 1.5 hours
Difficulty: Easy
High point: 60 feet
Elevation gain: 30 feet
Best hiking season: Year-round (but summer is hot)
Regulations: Dogs must be on leash and owners must pick up after
them; stay on designated trails
Map: The Memorial Park Conservancy Memorial Park
Contact: Houston Parks and Recreation Department, 713-845-1000,
www.memorialparkconservancy.org

Getting there: From the intersection of Interstate 10 and Loop 610,
take Loop 610 south 2.3 miles to the Memorial Drive exit. Head east on
Memorial Drive into the park and about a mile more to Picnic Loop and
turn right. Take an immediate right to the ball field parking lot.

Note: There are trash cans, restrooms, and a hose for doggie drinks and
rinsing off in the parking area. There is no clean water available on the
trail. Mosquitoes are abundant in this bayou-side park. Heavy rains can
close the trails. For conditions, call the Greater Houston Off-Road Biking
Association hotline, 713-437-6588.

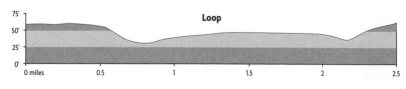

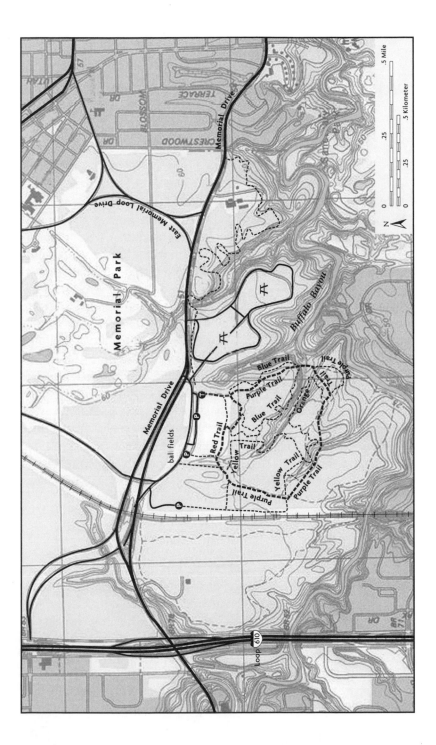

Brightly colored mushrooms pop up among the fallen leaves in Memorial Park.

Memorial Park is a green oasis in the middle of Houston, the country's fourth-largest city, and while much of it is heavily used and often crowded, time it right and you may have these trails almost to yourself. Half a dozen routes snake through a forested area bounded by Memorial Drive, the Southern Pacific Railroad, and Buffalo Bayou.

This hike follows the longest outer loop, designated by purple trail markers. It's a short jaunt along the left of the ball fields (as you are facing them) to the trail. Bear left when you hit the trail, which is a loose asphalt surface well padded with leaves and pine needles, to head clockwise around the loop. You will be following the outside of the trail area and generally avoiding any turnoffs, unless you and your dog feel like exploring. The wide, level trail is quite shady all year but still plenty hot in the summer as no breeze penetrates the thick vegetation. City sounds quickly give way to birdcalls and the occasional falling twig (dogs that like sticks will be in heaven). Keep to the right of the trail and be alert for bikes. But don't worry: Even midday on a Saturday, you will likely encounter only a dozen or so riders.

After about ten minutes of walking, the trail descends steeply to a creekbed that may or may not have water in it, depending on recent rains. It is usually easy to hop the small, muddy stream and head up the sandy slope on the other side. At the top, the trail forks; although both directions are marked orange, the left route is the Purple Trail. The slightly longer purple route goes closer to the bayou, but the Orange Trail to the right is narrower, with a sandy surface following the creekbed you just crossed. Take this more appealing alternative and in a few minutes you're back at the main Purple Trail, turning right to continue the loop. Watch for lichens, mushrooms, and American beautyberry, a lanky vinelike plant with clusters of small bright purple berries. The trees here include bald cypress, black cherry, loblolly pine, hawthorn, sycamore,

Vines spiral up many of Memorial Park's pines.

winged elm, yaupon holly, and a variety of oaks. Your dog will stay busy sniffing them all, along with numerous fallen limbs, which generally are left where they land.

The route passes two turnoffs for the Yellow Trail, and then you come to a major fork. Left leads to a dirt road in an open powerline right-of-way that offers sun, a breeze, and honeysuckle, wildflowers, butterflies, and dragonflies. If you go this way, turn right and follow the straight road to one of two cutoffs back to the main trail (if you reach a parking lot, you've gone too far). To stick with the purple loop, bear right at the fork. You'll pass another Yellow Trail crossing, then an intersection with the Red Trail. If you go straight here, you'll end up at the parking area on the opposite side of the ball fields from where you started, and you can cut across the open grass and the lot back to your car.

But it is more pleasant to turn onto the Red Trail, a narrow, sandy track that winds through tall pines. When the Red Trail forks, follow it right, down a deep muddy wash, then across a creekbed and a short boardwalk to the Blue Trail. Turn left here and you'll meet up with the Purple Trail and be back where you started. Take the short access trail back to your car, and get your dog a nice drink from the hose.

40. George Bush Park, Equestrian Center to Sports Park

Distance: 7 miles round trip
Hiking time: 3.5 hours
Difficulty: Easy
High point: 33 feet
Elevation gain: 5 feet
Best hiking season: Year-round (but summer is hot)
Regulations: Dogs must be on leash; scoop and pack out waste
Maps: USGS Clodine and Addicks 7.5' Quadrangles
Contact: Harris County Precinct 3 Parks, 281-496-2177,
   www.pct3.hctx.net/PGeorge

Getting there: From Loop 610 in Houston, follow Interstate 10 west to the exit to State Highway 6. Go left 3.4 miles to Westheimer, turn right, then right again almost immediately onto Westheimer Parkway, to enter the park. It is 2.6 miles to a turn for the equestrian center and hike and bike trail, then 0.8 mile to the parking lot.

Notes: Trail hours 7:00 AM to dusk. No services at trailhead. This trail is out in the open, and there is no water along the route.

Sometimes you just need to stretch all six of your legs, and this trail in 7800-acre George Bush Park is the place to do it. It is wide, straight, and flat with no roots, uneven patches, twists, or turns, so you can set a brisk pace, or bring a friend and have a nice, long conversation. Heck, you can even bring a friend in a wheelchair on this route. But don't come on a summer afternoon; there's precious little shade. There is also a shooting range nearby, and the sound follows you almost the entire hike—one way to find out if your dog is gun-shy.

From the equestrian center parking area, head back toward the road you drove in on toward the gate across the end of the road. The trail is asphalt, but this former roadbed also offers a loose dirt and gravel surface or even mowed grass on the sides that might be easier on the paws. For the first mile and a half, there are tall trees and thick brush on your right, and a semi-open meadow with scattered trees on your left. You'll see cardinals and other birds, even egrets when there is water in

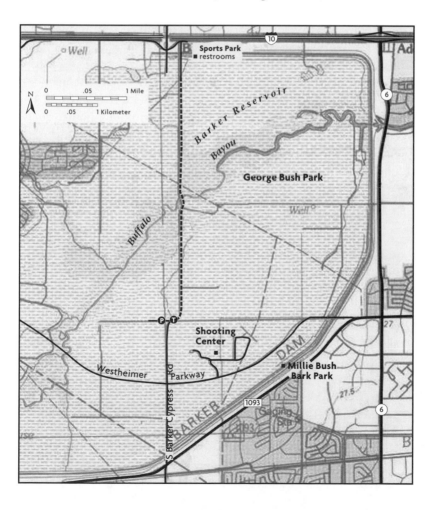

the ditches. At roughly the halfway point, you'll come to an old bridge over Buffalo Bayou.

The second half of the route has trees closer in, some even throwing shade on the path. Look for butterflies, dragonflies, palmettos, and gnarly old vine-covered trees with interesting holes in them. Benches at regular intervals on this part of the trail are good places for water breaks. At 2.7 miles, the hike and bike trail passes through another gate onto a narrow lane. You can turn around at the gate and retrace your steps or continue ahead (be aware of cows in the pasture to your right, which might spook your pup) and turn right after crossing a berm into the parking area for the Harris County Precinct 3 Sports Park, another 0.7 mile, where there are restrooms, water fountains, and a shower. You can also leave a car here if you want to avoid the backtracking (it will be safe, as this is also parking for county constables).

If you haven't worn your dog out yet, stop by the Millie Bush Bark Park—named for the "First Dog" under President George H. W. Bush—on Westheimer Parkway as you head back toward State Highway 6. It has separate areas for large and small dogs with swimming ponds, shade trees, a lot of open space, fake fire hydrants, and dog-level drinking fountains, all for free.

41. Lake Houston State Park, North River Trail

Distance: 7 miles round trip
Hiking time: 3 hours
Difficulty: Moderate
High point: 100 feet
Elevation gain: 40 feet
Best hiking season: Year-round (but summer is hot)
Regulations: Dogs must be on leash and are not allowed in Peach Creek; scoop and pack out waste
Map: Lake Houston State Park Trail Map
Contact: Lake Houston State Park, 281-354-6881, www.tpwd.state.tx.us/spdest/findadest/parks/lake_houston

Getting there: Take US Highway 59 north from Houston about 30 miles to the exit for New Caney and Lake Houston State Park, on Farm to Market

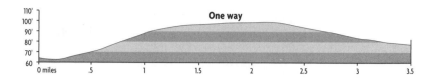

Road 1485. Turn right, go another 5.3 miles, turn right again onto Baptist Encampment Road (there is a sign to the park), and go 1.6 miles to the park entrance.

Notes: Entrance fee. The park is open year-round. Office hours are 8:00 AM to 5:00 PM; if you arrive before or after hours there is a self-pay "iron ranger" in the parking area. The headquarters has water fountains, and there is a vending machine across from the parking area. The park, located at the confluence of Caney Creek and the East Fork of the San Jacinto River, was once popular with bear hunters. Today, there are campsites, a sponsored-youth-group area, a group dining hall with a kitchen, a lodge that sleeps up to twenty-six with a fully equipped kitchen, and a cottage that sleeps twelve with a kitchen.

This is a long, peaceful walk through nearly 5000 acres of pineywoods to the East Fork of the San Jacinto River. Start at park headquarters, a short walk from the parking area. This is your chance to ask about trail conditions and check out the poster of poisonous snakes that call the park home. From here, take the paved path to Peach Creek. Cross the bridge, passing restrooms and through an open area, while following signs

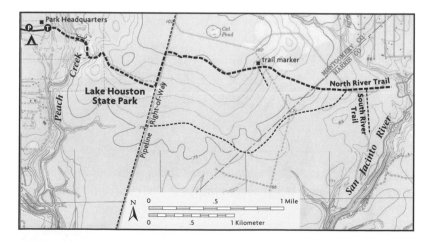

Several bridges traverse soft ground on the North River Trail near the San Jacinto River.

to the Hiking Trail, which leads into the trees. The sandy path winding through tall trees is covered with pine needles and exposed roots, fallen logs draped with velvety moss, and pinecones, some stripped down to the core.

You'll cross a horse trail and walk through more woods until, about a mile along, you reach a powerline right-of-way. Turn left here and follow the loose-gravel road about a half mile until the trail turns back into the trees. The trail is clearly marked with signs. From here, the trail is mowed grass, wide and level. Watch for large argiope garden spiderwebs strung across it. Most of them are above your head, but some may be at face level. The webs glow in the sunlight, which helps, and the spiders are eerily beautiful. You can count on plenty of other bugs in this lush woodsy environment—grasshoppers bursting up from the grass may startle your dog—but, thankfully, not too many mosquitoes. (Insect repellent is still a good idea, though, and be sure to spray around your ankles to keep away tiny critters waiting in the grass.)

Several trails lead off to your right, but stay to the left to keep heading toward the river. In addition to pines, magnolias, and other hardwood trees, look for American beautyberry and hummingbird vine. And keep a sharp eye out for poison ivy!

At about 2.5 miles, the trail forks, with one sign pointing to the North River Trail and the other to the South River Trail. Follow the North Trail to the left; it narrows here and you will probably see ample evidence of rooting pigs. You may even encounter the pigs themselves. Keep your dog under control and do not bother these wild animals, and they should pretty much ignore you or run away. After crossing a couple of wooden bridges, the trail narrows a bit more and, about a half mile along, dead-ends at a bluff over the San Jacinto River. There is a covered bench here from which to contemplate the languid muddy flow, or you can take a short jaunt, about 30 yards, to the right to a lower bank where you can reach the sandy shore. There is a current, so be careful about letting your pup swim, and the water is murky, so use your own judgment about letting her take a drink. A number of trees in this area have been stripped of bark in a 2-foot band all the way around and close to the ground, probably by beavers. You may see turtles and frogs, which you'll almost certainly hear, along with a multitude of birdcalls. Retrace your steps from here, and don't forget to stop off at Peach Creek—just don't let your dog swim in it.

42. Lake Livingston State Park

Distance: 3.5 miles round trip
Hiking time: 1.75 hours
Difficulty: Easy
High point: 150 feet
Elevation gain: 10 feet
Best hiking season: Year-round
Regulations: Dogs must be on leash; hiking is not allowed on the equestrian trail
Map: Texas Parks and Wildlife Lake Livingston State Park
Contact: Lake Livingston State Park, 936-365-2201,
www.tpwd.state.tx.us/spdest/findadest/parks/lake_livingston

Getting there: From Houston, take US Highway 59 north to Farm to Market Road 1988, 1 mile south of the town of Livingston. Turn left, go 4 miles, and turn right onto Farm to Market Road 3126; it is a half mile to the park entrance. Once inside the park, turn right at the intersection and drive to trailhead parking, next to the restrooms just past the horse stable.

Notes: Entrance fee. Restrooms at trailhead and several locations in campgrounds along the route. Lake Livingston is an 84,800-acre reservoir on the Trinity River, popular for fishing and boating. The park has campgrounds, boat ramps, fishing areas, a horse stable, a swimming pool, and hiking trails.

From the parking lot, walk to the left of the restrooms to pick up the trail. Or, if the trail is hard to make out due to fallen leaves and pine needles, walk to your right along the road and catch it between campsites 143 and 145, where it is more visible. This soft sand, pine-needle–covered trail meanders along the lakeshore through tall trees, passing through picnic areas and campgrounds with a jaunt into the woods at the other end. Nearly every step of the way is shaded by the towering loblolly pines

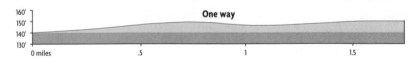

Lake Livingston State Park's trails are soft, pine-needle–covered sand under the shade of tall trees.

and water oaks, and dogs will enjoy sniffing at the numerous logs and the holes left behind by rooting armadillos. Humans can appreciate the gentle whisper of wind through thousands of pine needles and sunlight filtering through the forest canopy.

The first 1.5 miles or so are close to park roads, campgrounds, and the lake, so you may pick up the sound of an occasional car or boat, but except on the busiest summer weekends, this is a pretty peaceful hike. In the first half mile, the trail crosses an unused road, veers right toward the lake, then bisects a more open, windswept picnic area. It continues between a parking area on your left and a road, which leads to the park store and an observation tower, on the right. The trail is wider here and roughly follows the shore, although there are trees between you and the water. You'll see restrooms on your left and another boat ramp on the right, then cross a road and wander through picnic tables and more trees, passing a bridge to a trail heading off to the right. Keep going straight, cross another road, and pass a playground and a campground. The route is wide, smooth, and easy to follow here, crossing another road and passing between two camping areas before reaching a kiosk announcing that the next portion is the Harry F. McEwen and Stuart W. Moore Nature Trail. McEwen (1931–1997) was a soil scientist and active in the Boy Scouts. Moore (1982–2003) was a scout, became a Top Gun in the military, and died in Iraq.

This thumb-shaped trail takes you into thicker woods that are much more wild and tangled than those in the more developed part of the park. You will find more solitude here, as well as many fallen trees, including, sometimes, ones that have fallen over the trail. This section would form a loop, but a second bridge over an inlet of the lake is out, requiring you and your dog to retrace your steps back to the kiosk. From here, return to the trailhead the way you came.

If you would rather shuttle, you can park a car at the nearby boat ramp or at any of the day-use areas you passed on the way, but do not park in numbered camping spaces unless you have a camping permit for that space. Another option is to follow the park road back to your car, and if you do this, consider hiking the Pineywoods Nature Trail, a 1-mile loop that will be on the right more than halfway down the road back to the park entrance. This trail passes a duck pond, butterfly garden, and frog pond and crosses the equestrian trail several times. Occasional display boards provide information on the flora and fauna of the area, and there

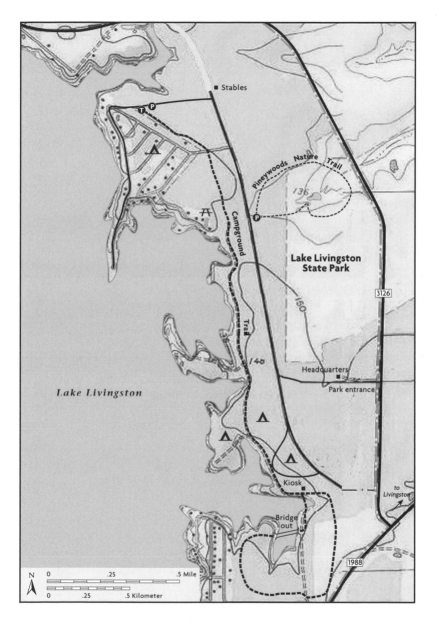

Stables

Pineywoods Nature Trail

Campground

Lake Livingston
State Park

3126

150

146

Headquarters

Park entrance

Lake Livingston

Kiosk

to
Livingston

Bridge
out

1988

N
0   .25   .5 Mile
0   .25   .5 Kilometer

are also benches, trash cans, and picnic tables along the way. The entire
route is on raised boardwalk, which may be frustrating for some dogs but
which makes this route fully accessible for the handicapped.

43. Lake Texana State Park, Trailhead 2

Distance: 4-mile loop
Hiking time: 2 hours
Difficulty: Easy
High point: 50 feet
Elevation gain: None
Best hiking season: Year-round
Regulations: Dogs must be on leash and should not be allowed in the water because of alligators; do not approach alligators; do not feed wildlife; store food inside vehicles
Map: Lake Texana State Park Hike and Bike Trails
Contact: Lake Texana State Park, 361-782-5718, *www.tpwd.state.tx.us/spdest/findadest/parks/lake_texana*

Getting there: From Houston, take US Highway 59 south 99 miles to Edna. Take State Highway 111 south from Edna 6.5 miles to the park entrance on your left.

Notes: Entrance fee. The park has camping and picnic areas, boat ramps, fishing piers, and fish cleaning stands, as well as trails.

Located halfway between Houston and Corpus Christi in the coastal vegetational region, this 525-acre park is mostly mixed oak and pecan woodlands that are common along the 74-mile Navidad River, which was dammed to create Lake Texana. White-tailed deer, squirrels, raccoons, rabbits, opossums, and armadillos are common, but visitors may also see skunks, turkeys, or even bobcats, as well as some 220 species of birds, a mixture of coastal prairie, hardwood bottomland, and riparian dwellers. This hike takes you through woodlands, more typical coastal grassland, and along some of the lakeshore.

Follow the main park road to Trailhead 2 parking. The route leads through low brush, across a wide pipeline easement, then into taller trees, the surface alternating between crushed granite and loose rock. Pass the turnoff for the footbridge to continue through the woods, roughly paralleling the shore of a lake inlet. As this inlet narrows, the trail veers to your left to meet up with the route from Trailhead 1. When you turn

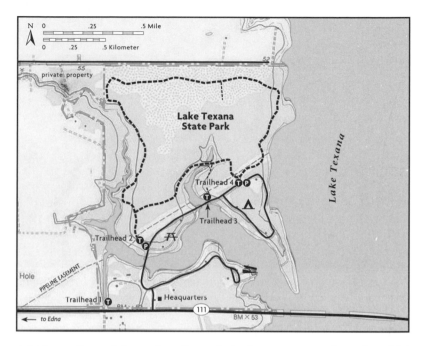

right here, the park boundary fence (private property on the other side) will be on your left for a short distance, then the trail goes right, eventually opening up to low, thick brush on either side. There are often deer tracks along the trail, as well as signs of armadillo rootings. You will pass a T intersection with a trail in from Trailhead 3 and will continue toward the main part of the lake. Here, the trail turns and roughly parallels the shore, but thick brush obscures most of the view and prevents access. Patches of tall trees here provide occasional shade, and debris and limbs on the ground indicate past flood levels and give your dog plenty to sniff. He may also be intrigued by the frequent sounds of rustling in the brush, which may be armadillos, squirrels, birds, or other animals.

You come to the pipeline easement again, which provides clear views of the lake, and follow the wide easement for a ways before meeting up with the Trailhead 4 trail. Take this to the right (the trailhead is just a short walk to the left), back across the easement, and to a left turnoff marked with a sign for the footbridge. This will take you through trees arching over the dirt path and through taller oaks to a wooden bridge over a finger of the lake. Look for turtles and lilies in the water.

From here, it is a pleasant walk among tall trees to where the trail reconnects with the way you came in. Turn left here and make your way

Thick brush forms an arch over the trail near the footbridge at Lake Texana State Park.

back to where you started. Deer often forage in the developed areas of the park; keep a tight hold on the leash and enjoy watching them, but remember not to feed any wildlife.

44. Huntsville State Park

Distance: 7.7-mile loop
Hiking time: 4 hours
Difficulty: Easy to moderate
High point: 350 feet
Elevation gain: 30 feet
Best hiking season: Year-round (but summer is hot)
Regulations: Dogs must be on leash and are not allowed in the lake
Map: Huntsville State Park Trail Map
Contact: Hunstville State Park, 936-295-5644,
www.tpwd.state.tx.us/spdest/findadest/parks/huntsville

Getting there: From Houston, take Interstate 45 north to the park exit, 6 miles before the town of Huntsville. Turn left onto Park Road 40 (under the highway) and continue into the park. Park at the nature center.

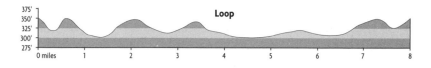

Notes: Entrance fee. Alligators are occasionally seen in the lake. There are restrooms and water at the nature center. The park also has camping, picnic areas, boat ramps, fishing piers, fish cleaning facilities, playgrounds, and horseback riding.

Huntsville State Park opened in 1938, which makes it one of the oldest parks in Texas. The Civilian Conservation Corps built a dam just below where Little Chinquapin and Big Chinquapin Creeks join to form Prairie Branch, creating 210-acre Lake Raven, the park's centerpiece. After floods in 1940 caused severe damage to the dam, the park was closed until 1956, following engineering studies, construction of a new spillway and dam, and restocking of the lake. The age of the park and its location in the Sam

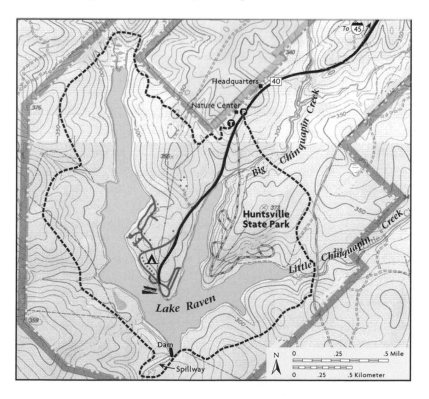

Debbie and Lexi pause on the boardwalk over a swampy part of the trail in Huntsville State Park.

Houston National Forest, near the western edge of the Southern Pine Belt, have allowed the loblolly and shortleaf pines here to grow to amazing heights. This hiking trail circles the lake, through these impressive woods and across swamps and streams. Nineteen wooden bridges along the way are numbered with plaques, and the numbers are also on the park's trail map, making it easy to track your progress. Start the hike just behind the nature center to follow the numbers in countdown fashion.

The sandy trail is punctuated with numerous roots, so step carefully, and the woods are full of scents to interest your dog. The trail hits a T intersection, where you will turn right, then cross another trail before coming to bridge number 19. Soon, you'll see swampy terrain on the left, then the trail turns that way and you and your pup will be crossing swampland on a boardwalk. Alligators do live in the park, so keep a tight hold on that leash, but you are more likely to see frogs and birds. After several more bridges, you are back to sandy trail winding through brush and trees, up and down some gentle hills. Once you cross bridge 12, the trail veers closer to the lake and then up onto the levee, and the campgrounds and other facilities are visible on the other side. You may also see, or hear, waterfowl on the lake.

When the trail takes a sharp right, the dam and spillway are visible straight ahead. Feel free to take a good look, but don't cross below the spillway; what look like steps are actually part of the dam structure, and they can be slippery and treacherous. Follow the trail as it makes a jog around the flow from the spillway, over three bridges, taking you to the opposite side of the dam. For a short distance, the trail follows an old asphalt road, then a sign directs you to turn left, back onto more familiar sand surface. Look for palmettos and American beautyberry among the brush, and the lake, now on your left, through the trees.

The route makes several turns, crosses a creek, then intersects a trail. Turn right at the next intersection (which has a bench), following the hiking trail signs. Bridge 3 crosses Little Chinquapin Creek, and a long boardwalk takes you over a slightly swampy area. Soon, the trail ends at the road across from the nature center where you started.

45. Brazos Bend State Park, Elm and 40-Acre Lake Trails

Distance: 4 miles round trip
Hiking time: 2 hours
Difficulty: Easy
High point: 65 feet
Elevation gain: 15 feet
Best hiking season: Year-round (but summer is hot)
Regulations: Dogs must be on leash; keep dogs away from the water
Map: Brazos Bend State Park Trails
Contact: Brazos Bend State Park, 979-553-5101,
   www.tpwd.state.tx.us/spdest/findadest/parks/brazos_bend

Getting there: From Houston, take US Highway 59 south to State Highway 288; go south, then west onto Farm to Market Road 1462. Follow 1462 to Farm to Market Road 762 south, which leads to the park entrance. Park at the nature center parking lot.

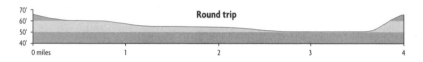

Round trip

70'
60'
50'
40'

0 miles   1   2   3   4

Notes: Entrance fee. Observe alligator etiquette. Do not throw objects into the water for your dog to retrieve or allow dogs to swim. Keep at least 30 feet from alligators. An outdoor guidebook available at the nature center (open weekends and most holidays 9:00 AM to 5:00 PM) contains information about the park's different ecosystems and relevant safety tips. The park also offers camping, picnicking, and fishing.

This hike combines loops around two of the park's lakes for a scenic route that practically guarantees alligator sightings. From the parking lot, look for the Pilant Slough Trail to the left of the amphitheater. This rock and caliche trail leads into wooded bottomland of sprawling oaks, snarly brush, and palmettos along the deep slough, passing a lot of moss-covered fallen trees and logs that dogs will want to sniff. A bench

Elm Lake in Brazos Bend State Park is home to alligators and other wildlife.

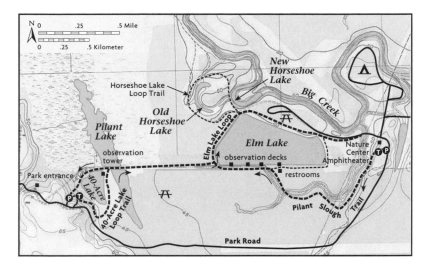

overlooking the slough is a good place to listen to the chorus of frogs that inhabit it and for some of the 270 species of birds that have been sighted in the park.

The trail then winds through open woods, where tall grass grows under trees wrapped with vines and draped with moss, before it dead-ends into the Elm Lake Loop. From the observation and fishing deck straight ahead, you likely will see alligators sunning themselves on the other side of the channel of water, herons searching for fish, and ducks paddling along the surface.

Turn left and follow the wide sand and gravel Elm Lake Loop along the shore of the reedy lake, passing a half dozen more of these decks over the water. At the end of the lake, the loop trail veers right, but continue straight toward the observation tower. The wide, tree-draped route crosses Pilant Lake, which is swampy at this point, to where the land and the water open up. A three-story observation tower located at the intersection of this trail and the 40-Acre Lake Loop Trail offers a 360-degree view of both 40-Acre and Pilant Lakes.

The hike then continues around to the right of 40-Acre Lake, where you will see and hear a plethora of ducks, egrets, herons, and other birds and may spot the occasional gator. The route passes a turnoff to Hoot's Hollow Trail, then the Prairie Trail, and crosses a parking lot, where there are restrooms, water, and a picnic area. Pick up the loop on the other side of the lot, where it veers through tall trees and giant vines and continues around the lake back to the tower.

The wide, tree-draped trail between Elm Lake and Pilant Lake is a good place to spot birds and, sometimes, alligators.

From here, retrace your steps to the Elm Lake Loop, where you will turn left to continue on that loop. At the next corner of the lake, the trail intersects the Horseshoe Lake Loop Trail, a 1.2-mile loop with another optional detour to the 1.9-mile Big Creek Loop Trail. Otherwise, turn right to continue following the shore of Elm Lake; the trail along this side passes through a tamer landscape of large, moss-draped oaks and mowed grass and close to a picnic area with restrooms. Some oaks in the park have been around since before Texas became a state.

At the far end of the lake, the loop trail bears right along the shore, leading back to where you first met up with it from the Pilant Lake Trail, but continue straight for the most direct route back to where you started. The trail parallels park road, with meadows on your right where you might spot deer or armadillos, before bringing you in on the other side of the nature center.

46. Big Thicket National Preserve, Sundew Trail

Distance: 1.5 miles
Hiking time: 45 minutes
Difficulty: Easy
High point: 138 feet
Elevation gain: Less than 10 feet
Best hiking season: Year-round
Regulations: Dogs must be on leash
Map: National Park Service Big Thicket Sundew Trail
Contact: Big Thicket National Preserve, 409-951-6725,
www.nps.gov/bith

Getting there: From Houston, take Interstate 10 east to Beaumont. Turn north (left) onto State Highway 69 and drive 35 miles to the Big Thicket National Preserve Visitor Center. From there, continue 6.7 miles north on State Highway 69 and turn left onto Farm to Market Road 2827, then left onto a dirt road, marked with a sign to the Sundew Trail parking lot.

Notes: No entrance fee, but hikers are requested to register at the trailhead. Insect repellent is recommended. There are restrooms across the parking area.

The Big Thicket National Preserve, the first preserve in the National Park System, is 97,000 acres on nine land units spread over 50 square miles in seven counties. Ten well-defined habitats are the result of a convergence of eastern hardwood forests, Gulf coastal plains, and Midwest prairies. In 1981, Big Thicket was designated an International Biosphere Reserve by the United Nations, part of a worldwide system of biosphere reserves.

This trail is located in the Hickory Creek Savannah Unit, which is less than one thousand acres. Wetland savannahs form where depressions in higher ground collect rainwater (average annual precipitation here is 55 inches). The landscape is characterized by open grassy flatlands and scattered longleaf pines, with a variety of grasses, sedges, rushes, and wildflowers. The blooming season for wildflowers in the area runs from February through November, and some of the many species you will see are rose gentians, gay feathers, and meadowbeauty. Several spe-

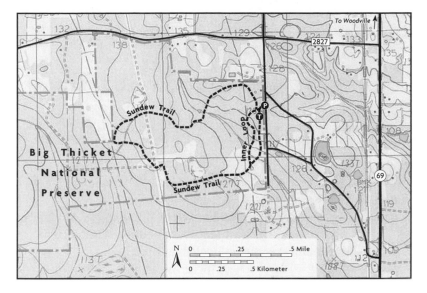

cies of orchids, and at least four species of carnivorous plants are also common here. These plants have evolved to eat insects to survive in the nutrient-poor soil created by the impenetrable clay hardpan below the surface in this area. Look for pitcher plants, which have narrow, funnel-shaped leaves with a rolled opening designed to trap insects. The trail's namesake sundew plant is also carnivorous. These are tiny plants, often smaller than a dime, so you will have to look closely in the grass for red rosettes. In the summer, the plants have tiny white or pink flowers. Their leaves are covered with glands that produce sticky fluid, which traps insects like flypaper.

After registering at the kiosk and picking up a trail guide, follow the sand and pine-needle–strewn trail counterclockwise into the trees. The outer loop is 1 mile, the inner loop is 0.5 mile, and both are wheelchair accessible. The route winds through pines and around swampy areas, which you will traverse on boardwalks. There are benches about every 400 feet and a picnic table at roughly the halfway point. You can also find mushrooms in the grass, and will hear many birds in the canopy overhead. Look for the symbols on the trail that correspond with descriptions in the guidebook. At the end of the loop, return the guidebook to the kiosk.

Much of the Sundew Trail is boardwalk over the often-wet ground, where several species of carnivorous plants grow.

47. Big Thicket National Preserve, Woodlands Trail

Distance: 5.4 miles balloon loop
Hiking time: 2.7 hours
Difficulty: Moderate
High point: 250 feet
Elevation gain: 60 feet
Best hiking season: Year-round
Regulations: Dogs must be on 6-foot leash; all plants and animals are protected; do not collect specimens or disturb animals; pack out all trash and stay on designated trails
Map: National Park Service Big Thicket Woodlands Trail
Contact: Big Thicket National Preserve, 409-951-6725, *www.nps.gov/bith*

Getting there: From Houston, go north on US Highway 59 to Livingston and turn east (right) onto US Highway 190. Drive 12 miles to Farm to Market Road 1276, marked as the turnoff for Dallardsville/Big Sandy, and go about 3.5 miles to the trailhead parking lot. For the Big Thicket National Preserve Visitor Center, take Interstate 10 east from Houston to Beaumont. Turn north (left) onto State Highway 69 and drive 35 miles. The center is on the right at Farm to Market Road 420. From there, you can take Farm to Market Road 943 18.5 miles to Farm to Market Road 1276 and drive about 10.2 miles to the trailhead.

Notes: Visitors are requested to sign in at the trailhead. Insect repellent recommended. No drinking water available. Backcountry camping allowed in designated parts of the preserve, but there are no developed campgrounds. Call the preserve for permit information. There are picnic sites in many of the units, some with barbecue grills, and contained charcoal grills are allowed. Open fires and collecting wood are prohibited. Fishing is allowed in all the waters with a Texas fishing license. Swimming

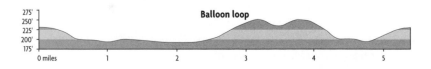

is allowed in the Neches River, but stay away from strong currents. In the summer, daytime temperatures are from the mid-80s to the mid-90s, but high humidity makes it feel much hotter. In the winter, the average daytime temperature is in the mid-50s. Rain is common year-round, so come prepared.

The Big Thicket National Preserve, managed by the National Park Service, was created to protect the complex biological diversity of a once-vast combination of pine and cypress forest, hardwood forest, meadow, and blackwater swamp. This unique area is created by the confluence of the southwest deserts, central plains, eastern forests, and southeastern swamps, where changes in elevation of a few feet can produce a dramatic change in vegetation. The biological diversity includes eighty-five tree species, more than sixty shrubs, twenty-six ferns, twenty orchids, and four carnivorous plants. Some 186 species of birds live here or migrate through, and there are fifty reptile species.

The preserve includes twelve scattered units covering 97,550 acres, and there are eight hiking trails, varying in length from about a mile up to 18 miles. The Woodlands Trail crosses a great variety of habitats, including the Big Sandy Creek floodplain and dense stands of hardwood. While the outer loop is 5.4 miles, there are two places where you can cut your hike to 3.3 or 4.5 miles.

The trail begins at a pine plantation planted around 1963 after the area was logged. A composting toilet and picnic tables are located here, along with an information kiosk with maps and the trail register. Once you leave the parking area, you and your dog immediately plunge into tall trees, then you skirt a pond that was built by a rancher in the area. The trail briefly follows an electric line, then heads once more into the trees. Wooden posts mark the trail, and at loop intersections, there are benches with a trail map engraved into them, so it is easy to find your route. The trail is generally easy to follow as well; however, when Hurricane Rita swept through here in the fall of 2005, her 100-mile-an-hour-plus winds wreaked significant damage on vegetation in the Big Thicket. On this hike, you will see hundreds of downed or broken trees, and while the National Park Service has cleared the trail, in some places, it was easier to create detours than to clear the trees. Your dog may find the large logs interesting places to explore, while you take a moment to appreciate the awesome power of nature. Some fallen trees have been down much longer, and you can see how quickly the forest reclaims these.

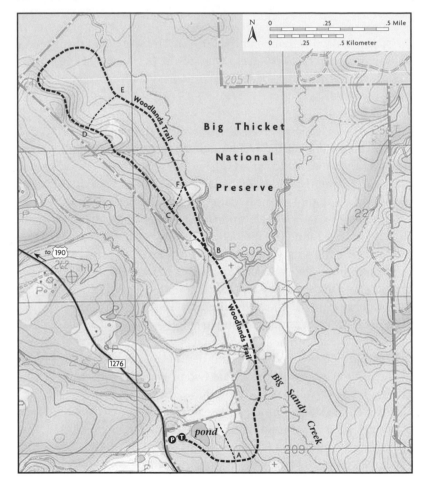

As the trail winds through the woods, it drops into the Big Sandy Creek floodplain, where the canopy becomes denser and there is less ground vegetation. There are sweet gum (look for abundant "gumballs," the round, hard, and prickly fruit of this tree, scattered on the ground), water oak, tupelo, and basket oak trees, many of them snarled in twisty vines. You will also see holly and hornbeam and bamboo. Thanks to local Boy Scout troops, there are boardwalks over many of the low areas, but you may still encounter wet trail. If the streams are flooded, do not try to follow a submerged trail, as you could step into a deep waterhole. The trail is mostly dirt or sand and is often scattered with leaves and pine needles, with some grassy areas. You are likely to see the tracks of coyote, deer, and other animals in the soft dirt.

Rain, a common occurrence in the Big Thicket National Preserve, doesn't deter Holly from a hike.

After about 1.3 miles, the trail forks at a post marked B. Stay to the right to continue roughly parallel to Big Sandy Creek. Watch for roots across the trail and cypress knees protruding from the ground, many of them green with moss. In a little more than 0.3 mile you will reach marker F, where a cross trail allows you to cut your hike short, if you must. If you continue on the outer loop, it is another 0.5 mile of winding along the creek to the next shortcut at marker E. The benches at these intersections are a good place to spend a moment listening and looking for birds.

Soon, the trail winds away from the creek, heading up a slope where you will see beech, magnolia, and loblolly pine. The trail follows the top of the slope for a ways, rising and falling some as it winds through the thick woods. When you cross a deep wash on a short bridge, look for the ferns and moss covering the sides of the slopes. There are large swaths of downed trees in this area, with some trail detours. Trees that have been down a longer time may be covered in colorful lichens. You pass the intersections with the two shortcuts, marked D and C on this side, then hike another 0.2 mile back to where the trail forked. On your way back, there is a short detour out to the pond, at marker A. There is another short trail out to the pond just before you reach the parking area on the main trail.

In addition to this trail and the Sundew Trail (Hike 46), the Big Thicket National Preserve has six other trails you may want to check out. The Kirby Nature Trail in the Turkey Creek Unit is a 2.4-mile outer loop and 1.7-mile inner loop through bald cypress swamps and other environments. Also in that unit is the 15-mile Turkey Creek Trail, which parallels the creek of the same name, with access at four trailheads. On the northeast side of that trail is a 0.2-mile loop, the Pitcher Plant Trail, where you and your dog can find carnivorous pitcher plants. Beaver Slide Trail in the Big Sandy Creek Unit is a 1.5-mile trail around a series of ponds formed by old beaver dams. The Beech Woods Trail is a 1-mile loop in the Beech Creek Unit, and the Big Sandy Creek Horse/Bike Trail is the longest at 18 miles and crosses upland pine forests and beech/magnolia/loblolly pine slopes as well as a floodplain forest. These last two trails are closed during hunting season—call for exact dates—and, as its name indicates, horseback riders and cyclists also use the Big Sandy Creek Horse/Bike Trail. A guidebook and maps are available from the visitor center.

48. Sam Houston National Forest, Lone Star Hiking Trail

Distance: 27 miles one way
Hiking time: 16.5 hours
Difficulty: Moderate
High point: 90 feet
Elevation gain: 40 feet
Best hiking season: Fall through spring
Regulations: Dogs must be on leash; pack out all trash and waste
Map: U.S. Forest Service Sam Houston National Forest
Contact: Sam Houston National Forest, 936-344-6205, *www.fs.fed .us/r8/texas/recreation/sam_houston/samhouston_gen_info.shtml*

Getting there: Take Interstate 45 north from Houston to State Highway 150 at New Waverly. Go east on State Highway 150 approximately 19 miles

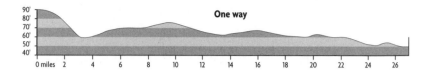

to Farm to Market Road 945, and turn right. Trailhead parking will be about 2 miles down on the left at National Forest Road 2126 (dirt road). To reach the terminus trailhead, take Interstate 45 north to Conroe, then State Highway 105 east to Cleveland and turn north onto Farm to Market Road 1725 to the trailhead. From here, return to Cleveland and go north on US Highway 59 a short distance to Farm to Market Road 2025. Go north, and turn left onto Farm to Market Road 945 to the trailhead, on your right (if you reach State Highway 150, you've gone too far).

Notes: Some parts of the trail flood in wet weather, and stream crossings without bridges can be dangerous. Call for trail conditions before heading out. Camping is allowed anywhere along the trail except during deer hunting season, generally November through January (exact dates vary, so call ahead), when camping is restricted to designated camping areas. There is a full-service campground at the Double Lake Recreation Area and several primitive campsites with no facilities. Use only dead and down wood for campfires, and be sure all fires are completely out and covered with dirt before leaving. During hunting season, hikers should wear highly visible clothing, preferably something in hunter orange.

The Lone Star Hiking Trail runs 128 miles through the Sam Houston National Forest, from Lake Conroe to near Cleveland. The 27-mile section from the trailhead on Farm to Market Road 945 to the terminus near Winters Bayou Scenic Area on Farm to Market Road 1725 is a designated National Recreation Trail. Five access points allow you to choose a shorter route or to break the hike into two days. The natural trail is generally only a narrow path through the forest, mostly sandy, with some grassy stretches. In many places, thick roots make careful footing necessary, especially when leaves and pine needles have covered the trail. Hikers can spot white-tailed deer, turkey, quail, and dove. Rabbits, foxes, and bobcats also live in the pineywoods. Other residents include mosquitoes, ticks, and chiggers, so insect repellent is recommended, especially in the summer.

The entire Lone Star Trail, including this section, is well marked with 2-by-4-inch aluminum tags placed on trees about 25 to 50 yards apart. A tag posted with the 4-inch side straight up and down indicates that

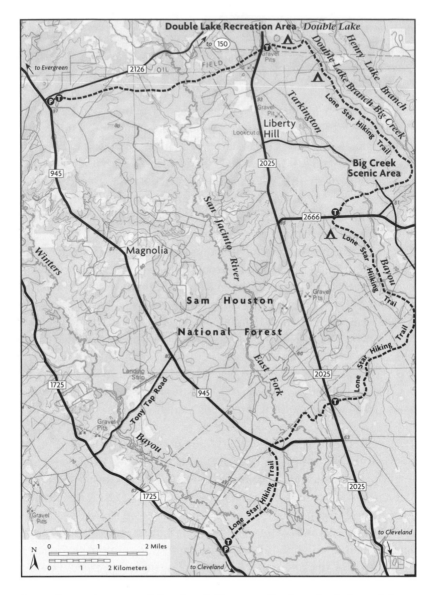

the trail continues straight ahead. Tags are tilted to the left or right to indicate turns in the trail, with double tilted tags meaning a sharper turn. In the past, triangular markers were used, and some of these may still be seen. There are often trees down across the trail, requiring you and your dog to detour. Just look across the obstacle and ahead for the next markers to get back on the trail. In the fall, leaves can obscure the trail, too, but again, just keep looking ahead for the markers. A map is highly recommended.

The section from Farm to Market Road 945 to Double Lake is called the Magnolia Section, and in addition to pines, you will see many magnolia trees. The trail here is often through thick brush over your head on either side, along with more open areas. You will see a swampy area on your left and large, open pastureland not far from the trail, and you will cross a couple of creeks. After 3.7 miles, the trail crosses the East Fork of the San Jacinto River, little more than a wide creek at this point. (Floods from Hurricane Rita washed out the bridge in September 2005; replacement was anticipated by fall 2006.)

The trail follows the river for a ways, then meanders along one of its tributaries before heading uphill a bit and crossing Farm to Market Road 2025 (you have now gone about 6 miles). There are hiker gates near the trail access points, and you pass through one here into what is known as the Big Creek Scenic Section. In 1.2 miles the trail veers to Double Lake, which has a campground with restrooms, showers, and water. In the summer, a concession stand is open.

From here, the trail roughly follows Big Creek, which has water year-round, about 4 miles to the Big Creek Scenic Area. This aptly named area is one of the most scenic of the hike. Your dog will enjoy exploring the bases of trees that have fallen over, pulling up large sections of the sandy ground with their roots. There are several footbridges across swampy areas or smaller creeks. Old stumps are covered in moss of various shades of green, as are fallen logs, which often have strangely shaped fungi growing on them. Mushrooms of different sizes and colors are also plentiful along the trail, but you will have to look for them. In one swampy area, there is a thick patch of thorny plant aptly named devil's walkingstick.

At about 11.5 miles, the trail intersects with one end of the Big Creek Trail, which comes in from a parking area on County Road 217. There are several loop trails in this area, indicated with orange tape strips on the metal markers. The main trail follows an old road along a raised area and is almost straight for several miles. You will pass the other end of Big Creek Trail and a sign with a map of the Big Creek Scenic Area, showing all the loop trails. The Big Creek trailhead is off to your left here.

Soon, you cross a gravel road, then a creek, and then come to a trailhead at Farm to Market Road 2666, which you will cross and follow briefly before the trail heads south again. The trail follows Tarkington Bayou for a distance, then turns southwest, reaching Farm to Market Road 2025

Crossing Winters Bayou on the Lone Star Hiking Trail.

again at roughly 23 miles. Cross the road and follow the trail downhill, across a stream, and back uphill, winding around through trees, then up onto a levee for a while, with very wet areas on either side. Cross a bridge, then follow a dirt road a short distance before turning back into the woods. You will once again cross the San Jacinto River, then Farm to Market Road 945.

In this area, you will see the concrete bases of old fire towers and cross several gravel roads and streams. There is a high bridge over Winters Bayou, which always has water, and the trail passes under a powerline. In this wet area, palmetto plants are abundant under the tall trees. There are several other footbridges, and you continue winding through the pines and palmettos before reaching the end of the trail at Farm to Market Road 1725.

THE SHORE

49. Crystal Beach

Distance: 4–4.5 miles one way
Hiking time: Varies
Difficulty: Easy
High point: 5 feet
Elevation gain: None
Best hiking season: Year-round
Regulations: Dogs must be on leash on Galveston County beaches (although some sources say otherwise)
Maps: USGS Flake and Caplen 7.5' Quadrangles
Contact: Crystal Beach Convention and Visitors Bureau, 409-684-5940

Getting there: From Houston, take Interstate 45 south to Galveston. From Galveston, catch the Bolivar Ferry at the east end of Galveston Island.

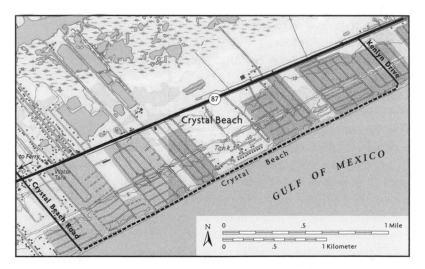

A quick dip in the warm Gulf of Mexico leaves Keeper ready for more hiking.

Once you exit the ferry, continue on State Highway 87 for 15 miles and turn right onto Crystal Beach Drive (there is a signal light), which dead-ends on the beach.

Notes: The ferry and parking on the beach are free. Beach rules prohibit littering, glass containers, and bonfires, as well as driving on the dunes. On the way back to the ferry, stop at Fort Travis County Park, where there are restrooms and shower facilities. There are no services on the beach.

There are 27 miles of beach on the Bolivar Peninsula and four communities, beginning with Port Bolivar closest to the ferry, then Crystal Beach, Gilchrist, and High Island. All are unincorporated, so the beaches on the peninsula are under the jurisdiction of Galveston County. Crystal Beach begins about 6.5 miles from the ferry and extends for about 7 miles. This beach is seldom crowded, except during the summer months, and the only development is groups of colorful beach houses perched on stilts behind the dunes. With low, grassy dunes on one side and the shallow water and gentle waves on the other, you and your dog can keep an eye out for the occasional seashell or rare sand dollar without worrying about getting lost. The sand is generally compacted, which allows for fast walking if that's your bent. Just keep an eye on your dog in case she discovers a smelly fish carcass, and stay out of the fragile dunes (where there are snakes and mosquitoes anyway). Although cars can drive on the beach, they are usually moving at a slow pace (the speed limit is 15 mph).

For a hike of some 4 miles, head north on the beach from Crystal Beach Drive to Kenlyn Drive and then back. Or keep going, either way, if you and your dog have a lot of energy left—just remember to save enough for the hike back. There is almost always a stiff sea breeze, and the shallow, warm water feels good on feet and paws alike.

50. Galveston Island State Park, Bayou Trails

Distance: 4 miles round trip
Hiking time: 2 hours
Difficulty: Easy
High point: 5 feet
Elevation gain: None
Best hiking season: Spring through fall
Regulations: Dogs must be on leash; walk only on designated footpaths; remove all trash and dog waste
Map: Texas Parks and Wildlife Galveston Island State Park
Contact: Galveston Island State Park, 409-737-1222, *www.tpwd.state.tx.us/spdest/findadest/parks/galveston*

Getting there: From Houston, take Interstate 45 south to Galveston, and exit right onto Sixty-first Street and continue south to Seawall Boulevard (Farm to Market Road 3005). Turn right and drive 10 miles to the park entrance. Turn left into the park to obtain an entrance permit; the trail is across Farm to Market Road 3005. Drive past the interpretive center, take the first left, and drive about three-tenths of a mile to the Clapper Rail Trail parking area.

Notes: Insect repellent is highly recommended for this area. The park closes during hurricane watches or warnings, so call ahead June through November or check the website. The hiking trails are on the bay side, but facilities (restrooms, water fountains) are located in the beachside area of the park.

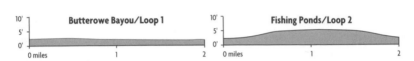

Galveston Island is about 5000 years old and has a rich history; explorer Cabeza de Vaca was shipwrecked here in 1528, when he encountered the native Karankawas, who had disappeared as a distinct tribe by 1860. In 1817, pirate Jean Lafitte raided Spanish ships from outposts he built here with the blessing of Mexican revolutionaries, for obvious reasons. A hurricane in 1900 killed 5000 to 10,000 people and motivated construction of the city's 7-mile-long seawall.

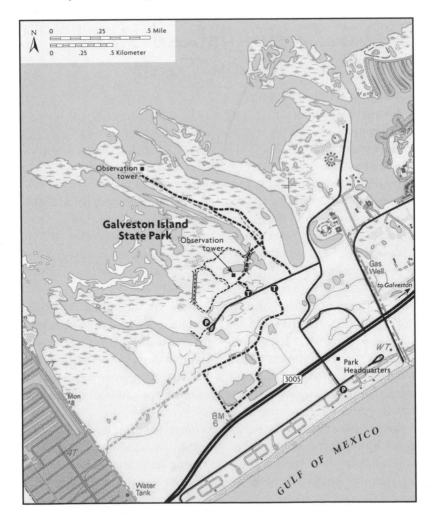

Barrier islands like Galveston are transitions between land and ocean and support a variety of distinct ecoregions, including prairie and salt marsh wetlands, which this hike traverses. The park staff have been working to eliminate invasive plants and restore native vegetation such as gulf cordgrass and switchgrass. The area around the marsh supports coyotes, opossums, rabbits, snakes, raccoons, and armadillos; spotted sea trout, red drum, flounder, blue crab, and shrimp live in the marsh, where they attract birds like great blue herons, snowy egrets, roseate spoonbills, and mottled and mallard ducks.

From the parking lot, it is a short walk on mowed grass to an observation tower with a ramp rather than stairs, making it easy for you and your dog to climb up and get your bearings. From here, you can see a second observation tower in the distance that you will reach on this hike. From the first tower, head to your right (as you face the bay away from the road) and cross two boardwalks, where jumping fish will get your dog's attention. Turn left immediately after crossing the second one (this trail will be soggy after rains) and walk toward the next tower, with Butterowe Bayou on the left and brush on the right. Most of the year, wildflowers are sprinkled generously among the grasses, and birds and dragonflies are abundant.

This part of the trail is a loop with an out-and-back spur to the second tower. Keep going straight to the tower, about another quarter mile, then retrace your steps back to the loop and bear left to continue through tall grasses and brush. The loop closes just a bit farther down than where you turned to start, but continue straight here to the road you drove in on. You have now hiked about two miles, and can walk along the road all the way back to your car, or go just about one-tenth of a mile and turn left onto a wide, mowed route for another loop of about two miles. Mushrooms sprout on the trail, and patches of cattails grow in the tall brush alongside it.

About a half mile along, take the left at a fork in the trail to start the loop. The trail passes several ponds, good places to see birds like roseate spoonbills and hummingbirds. If your dog will sit quietly, spend a few minutes in one of the photography blinds for a closer look. You can fish in these ponds, but alligators call them home, too, so keep your dog on leash and out of the water.

The trail leads to a parking area, where you turn right and hike straight ahead to continue the loop. Another mile or so and you reach the intersection with the way you came in. Retrace your steps to your car. If

The lush native vegetation of the marsh wetland in Galveston Island State Park supports a variety of wildlife.

you continue down the road past the parking lot, it is about a tenth of a mile to an oak motte where, from January to June, you may see a pair of crested caracaras that have nested here for a number of years.

51. Brazoria National Wildlife Refuge, Big Slough Trail

Distance: 1-mile loop
Hiking time: 45 minutes
Difficulty: Easy
High point: 5 feet
Elevation gain: None
Best hiking season: Fall through spring
Regulations: Dogs must be on leash; scoop and pack out waste
Map: Brazoria National Wildlife Refuge Big Slough Trail Guide
Contact: Texas Mid-Coast National Wildlife Refuge Complex,
979-849-6062, *www.fws.gov/southwest/refuges/texas/texasmidcoast*

Getting there: Take State Highway 288 south from Houston to Angleton, and turn left onto Farm to Market Road 523 and drive to County Road 227. Turn left and drive 1.7 miles to the refuge entrance on your right. It is 3 miles from there to the Discovery Center.

Notes: Mosquito repellent is essential for man and beast. It is hot and sunny here much of the year; carry adequate water as it is not a good idea

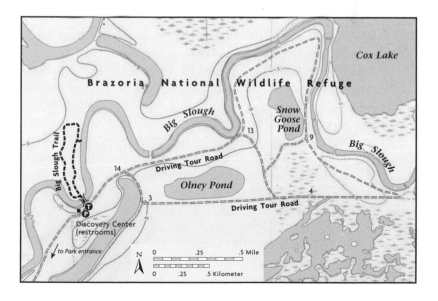

An observation platform over Big Slough is a good place to search for birds and other denizens of the refuge.

for your dog to drink from the ponds and sloughs (think alligators). The Discovery Complex has exhibits and information, as well as restrooms, water fountains, and shade. The center is generally open 7:30 AM to 4:00 PM during winter months, the refuge's busy season.

This wildlife refuge, along with the nearby San Bernard and Big Boggy refuges, provides vital coastal wetlands for migrating waterfowl in winter and is an entry point for songbirds migrating across the Gulf of Mexico. The salt and freshwater marshes, sloughs, ponds, coastal prairies, and bottomland forest create great opportunities for wildlife watching. Brazoria's 5000-acre native bluestem prairie is one of the last in Texas.

Pick up a Big Slough (pronounced *slew*) trail guide in the Discovery Center building or from the Information Pavilion (covered picnic table just to the right of and behind the building). This is also where the trail starts. The first portion is boardwalk over the slough, which stretches some 20 miles, where open freshwater mingles with rushes, marsh grasses, cattails, and water lilies. A shady bench makes a good spot to look for frogs, turtles, herons, and, yes, alligators.

After the boardwalk, bear right on the mowed grass and gravel trail through mostly open terrain with occasional trees that provide welcome shade. Watch for spiderwebs across the trail, listen for the sounds of birds, and observe the seasonal wildflowers and their attendant butterflies. There is an observation platform over the slough, surrounded by cattails, a good spot to linger and observe. Be careful of snakes, as cottonmouth and rattlesnakes do appear here, although more common are rat and water snakes, which eat small rodents. Snakes may be sunning on the trail on wet days but are most likely buried in the mud when it is hot. Bats, purple martins, chimney swifts, and dragonflies are here to take advantage of the abundant mosquito buffet. Cardinals and mockingbirds are common sights and, in the spring and summer, you may hear quail or startle a flock of them from the undergrowth. Other wildlife you might get a chance to see if your dog is quiet and you are patient are coyotes and feral hogs, which enjoy cooling off in the mud. The hogs are formerly domestic animals that have gone wild, and they are a threat to the habitat and native wildlife. Do not approach or disturb wild hogs.

Continue on the outer loop, avoiding shortcuts bisecting the circle that lead off to your left. In fall and winter, there are thousands of migrating birds at Brazoria; an annual Christmas bird count by the Audubon Society regularly finds more than two hundred species on the refuge. To increase your chances of seeing more birds, take time to sit quietly (assuming you brought mosquito repellent) on one of the dozen or so benches scattered along the trail.

The refuge also offers a 7.5-mile driving tour that you and your dog are welcome to do on foot. Pick up an auto tour map at the Information Pavilion to plan your route. The tour circles several large ponds that host waterfowl and shorebirds, and several crossover points make it possible to adjust your distance. From the parking area, follow the auto tour markers, turning right at the first fork to marker 3, skirting Olney Pond, where millet attracts snow geese and ducks, to the next intersection, at which point you can continue ahead or turn left to circle the pond. In addition to waterfowl of all types and wading birds such as spoonbills and avocets, you can spy hawks and other birds of prey in the sky or on poles and fence posts along this walk. Where this shortcut dead-ends at marker 13, you can take a short walk to the right to an observation platform over Teal Pond, which has a telescope and interpretive displays, then continue on to circle that pond (just keep turning right until you are back at marker 13), or retrace your steps from the platform back to marker 13 and on around Olney Pond back to where you parked.

Another option is to walk the 1.5-mile gravel road across from the Discovery Complex, which leads south to the Salt Lake Fishing Area. Along this straight, open road, you'll pass an alligator pond and abundant wildflowers and other vegetation and will see a lot of dragonflies and birds.

52. Padre Island National Seashore

Distance: Up to 120 miles
Hiking time: Varies
Difficulty: Easy to moderate
High point: Sea level
Elevation gain: None
Best hiking season: Spring through fall
Regulations: Dogs must be on leash except when swimming; pack out all trash and dog waste; camping permit required
Map: National Park Service Padre Island National Seashore
Contact: Padre Island National Seashore, 361-949-8068, *www.nps.gov/pais*

Getting there: From Corpus Christi, take State Highway 358 toward Padre Island and across the bay, then continue south on State Highway 358, which becomes Park Road 22, about 11 miles to the park entrance.

Notes: Entrance fee. The visitor center is open every day except December 25. Tides, weather, and beach conditions can be obtained day and night at 361-949-8175. The Malaquite Pavilion has a bathhouse, park store, water fountains, visitor center, first aid, and public telephone. Dogs are not allowed in this area, but there is an outdoor shower near the end of the boardwalk where you can wash the sand from your companion's fur. Campsites and primitive camping are available (obtain permits at the visitor center). No camping in the dunes, grasslands, or mudflats. All campers can use the showers and toilets at Malaquite Pavilion, which are open all night.

It is hard to believe there is still a beach in this country that stretches for 60 undisturbed miles, with nary a condo or bar in sight. But here it is, the longest stretch of undeveloped barrier island in the world (ending at the human-made Mansfield Channel more than 60 miles south of

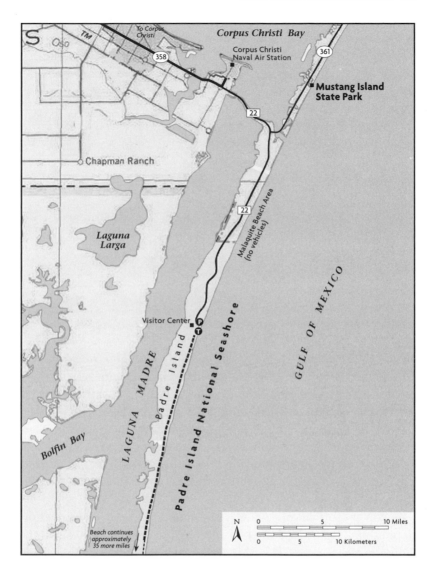

here). You're not likely to want to walk the entire length with your dog, but it is nice to know you could. You will probably want to stick to the section between mileposts 0 and 5, where you can drive your vehicle on the beach. It is strictly four-wheel-drive territory after milepost 5, with mile markers every 5 miles. Walk as far as you like, but expect isolation, mosquitoes, and no services.

Another option is Malaquite Beach, a stretch of about 4 miles where

Vines and other native vegetation crown Padre Island's dunes.
(Photo courtesy of the National Park Service)

no vehicles are allowed. Most of the people on Malaquite Beach tend to be close to the visitor center, or in the first mile or so of the open beach, where you will find tents, RVs, and a lot of dogs. There is no path per se; just sand and more sand, loose near the dunes and more packed, although irregular, near the water. Gulls, pelicans, crabs, seaweed, and detritus are all delicious distractions for a dog, so you won't make good time unless your dog is very focused. But then, who wants to make good time on a beach?

Follow the surf line on your way out, cooling feet and paws from time to time, and exploring driftwood and puddles, then hike closer to the dunes on the way back. These are covered with sea oats, bluestem grass, goatfoot morning glory vines, and other native plants that help stabilize the dunes. Rattlesnakes frequent this area, so it is important not to tramp around on the dunes and vegetation. This will be easy as your dog will be on a leash unless he is swimming (outside the Malaquite Beach area, dogs can swim in the water leash free). Remember to carry fresh water for both of you and plenty of sunblock.

Endangered sea turtles nest on Padre Island's beaches from March to September. If you see a nesting mother turtle, remain at least 20 feet away until she has begun laying eggs. If you come too close, she may interrupt the process and return to the water without laying her eggs. Once she has finished and left, you may approach closer and mark the nest with material from the beach (do not stick objects into the sand) and report the sighting to a park ranger at 361-949-7163, extension 0. Do not let your dog disturb turtles or nests. Do not trample the loose sand above the eggs or they could smother. Padre Island is also in the Central Flyway, a migration route followed by birds between South America and the Arctic, so in spring and fall take time to watch for birds. In the fall look for peregrine falcons and in winter a variety of migrating hawks. Laughing gulls, terns, brown pelicans, and great blue herons hang around all year.

53. Matagorda Island Wildlife Management Area

Distance: 6 miles round trip
Hiking time: 3 hours
Difficulty: Easy
High point: 10 feet
Elevation gain: None
Best hiking season: Fall through spring
Regulations: Hiking, bird watching, and biking are allowed on the north end of the island (from the runway/headquarters complex, down the road system to the lighthouse and including the beach) during daylight hours. These activities are not allowed during public hunts. All trash must be taken with you from the island.
Map: Texas Parks and Wildlife Matagorda Island Wildlife Management Area
Contact: Matagorda Island Wildlife Management Area, 979-244-6804, *www.tpwd.state.tx.us/huntwild/hunt/wma/find_a_wma/list/?id=48*

Getting there: Take US Highway 59 south from Houston to Victoria (about 120 miles), then State Highway 185 south to Port O'Connor. Matagorda Island is approximately 7 miles from the mainland across San Antonio and Espiritu Santo Bays and accessible only by boat. Shuttle service to the island can be arranged in Port O'Connor; call the parks office or the Port O'Connor Chamber of Commerce, 361-983-2898, for

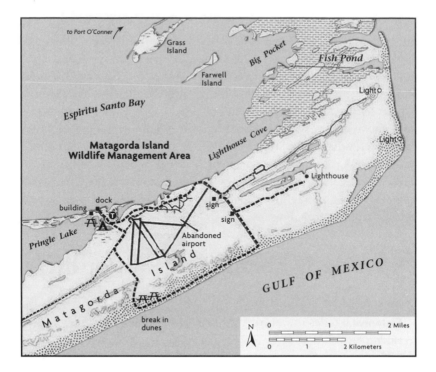

a list of licensed guides. Know in advance whether your dog is comfortable riding in boats!

Notes: A permit, which can be obtained from local license vendors, is required for hiking and primitive camping.

This loop hike of roughly 6 miles goes from the bayside boat dock to the beach, along the shore, and back, with an optional detour to the Matagorda Lighthouse. Thanks to the inaccessibility of this barrier island, you and your dog are likely to have the hike, and in fact the entire place, to yourselves. If you hired a guide to bring you to the island, be sure to make arrangements for a pickup time. If you come in your own boat, allow plenty of time to return to the mainland before dark, unless you are camping. There are picnic tables, running water (not potable), and restrooms at the bayside dock, and picnic tables on the beach. Camping is allowed in both locations.

Approximately 44,000 acres of the island are a wildlife management area, and the U.S. Fish and Wildlife Service manages another 11,500 acres on the south end of the island. So this is a haven for birds and wildlife, and hikers are likely to see quail, redwing blackbirds, pelicans, deer, and other animals, including 29 endangered or threatened species that live here. The park started a program to reintroduce endangered aplomado falcons in 2001, and now there are many nesting pairs on the island. Look for them on the old utility poles.

Head east from the boat dock area and bear left, after passing the sign and some palm trees, along an old road that roughly parallels the shore along the bay. Soak up the sun and solitude, watching windswept sea grasses and listening to the distant roar of surf. A half-dozen scattered palms rattle in the wind, punctuated by the call of birds in the brush and flying overhead. After passing a couple of old water tanks on the left, bear in that direction, continuing to parallel the shore. A swampy area thick with reeds on the right is alive with the chatter of frogs. The pavement gives way to mowed grass with occasional puddles if there has been any rain lately—fresh water that your dog can drink. The road crosses an old, overgrown cattle guard, then joins up with a shell road. A park sign directs you straight ahead to the lighthouse and Gulf of Mexico. Look for wildflowers in the thick, low brush, and expect to pull a lot of stickers from your dog's paws if she isn't wearing booties. Alligators and snakes (cottonmouths and rattlers) are other possible hazards here, so keep your pooch close and out of any water except shallow puddles.

A road forks to the left, but continue straight ahead to the turnoff for the lighthouse, which is marked, about a mile from here. The lighthouse was built in 1852, when some 160 people lived on the island in a tiny town called Saluria. During the Civil War, Fort Esperanza was hastily constructed on Matagorda Island to protect naval traffic, and in 1862, with Texas one of the last conduits of cotton out of the South, Union gunboats attacked and took over the island and fort. They soon departed, however, and were forced to retake the island from Confederate forces a year later, at heavy cost, only to have it recaptured by the South in 1864. The war took its toll on island residents, and a hurricane a few years later pretty much sealed the fate of Fort Esperanza and the town of Saluria. The lighthouse, entered into the National Registry of Historical Landmarks in 1984, fell into disrepair and the U.S. Coast Guard turned it off in 1995. A foundation was formed to save the lighthouse, which now shines with solar power. After admiring the restored old beacon, head back to where you turned off, go right, and continue to the beach.

At this point, you can retrace your steps to that first sign to the lighthouse and Gulf, and bear left to meet up with a wide, long runway,

Scattered palms tower above the windswept coastal landscape on Matagorda Island.

remnant of the island's days as a training ground for World War II pilots. Follow the runway to a paved turnoff, directly across from the park buildings near the dock, which you can clearly see, and continue to the old tarmac, overgrown by grasses along the pavement seams, creating a bizarre giant checkerboard. From here, follow any of the roads leading back to the dock. This will be about 3.5 miles.

Or, hike along the deserted beach for about 2.5 miles to partake in some of the best beachcombing available in Texas (do not collect any live shells, and don't overdo it). There will be plenty of interesting things for your dog to sniff, but watch for human debris that might include glass or sharp metal. If you see the remains of dolphins, sea turtles, or other marine life, do not disturb them, and report them to the park when you get back. Sea turtles nest on the island, so look for tracks or nests, which will look like circles of disturbed sand, and report those as well. When you reach an area with picnic tables and shelters, look for a turnoff through the dunes. Follow the dirt road to the other end of the old runway, turn right on it, and take any of the roads back to the dock and buildings.

54. Aransas National Wildlife Refuge, Dagger Point Trail

Distance: 1-mile loop
Hiking time: 30 minutes
Difficulty: Easy
High point: 25 feet
Elevation gain: 20 feet
Best hiking season: Fall through spring
Regulations: Dogs must be on leash; camping is not allowed
Map: U.S. Fish and Wildlife Service Aransas National Wildlife Refuge
Contact: Aransas National Wildlife Refuge, 361-286-3559,
   www.fws.gov/southwest/refuges/texas/aransas.html

Getting there: From Victoria, take US Highway 77 south to State Highway 239 and turn left. Stay on State Highway 239 in Tivoli and continue to Austwell, then take Farm to Market Road 2040 about 7 miles to the refuge entrance. From the visitors center, drive about 3 miles to the Dagger Point trailhead, well marked on the second left turnoff.

Notes: Entrance fee. Visitors are required to register at the visitors center. Alligators and poisonous snakes call the refuge home, as do mosquitoes, ticks, and chiggers. Bring insect repellent. Closest fuel is 14 miles away in Tivoli; other services are 35 miles away in Rockport (south) or Port Lavaca (north).

This 70,504-acre wildlife refuge is on the Blackjack Peninsula in the Gulf of Mexico. The landscape includes grasslands, oak mottes, redbay thickets, tidal marshes, freshwater ponds, and shores. Aransas is home to many creatures, including alligators, deer, bobcats, and more than 392 species of birds, including endangered whooping cranes, which winter here. The refuge offers a 16-mile auto tour loop, a 40-foot observation tower (good for viewing the cranes), picnic areas, and several trails. One of the longest trails is the 1-mile Dagger Point Trail, which traverses coastal forest and

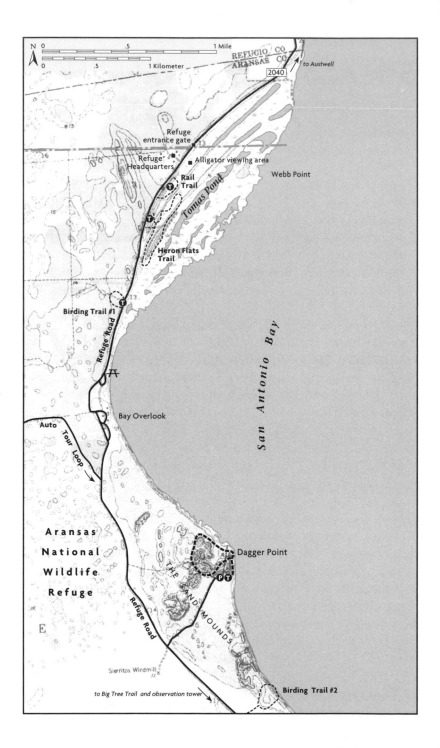

N 0   .5   1 Mile

0   .5   1 Kilometer

REFUGIO CO.
ARANSAS CO.

2040

to Austwell

Refuge
entrance gate   13

16

Refuge
Headquarters

Alligator viewing area

Webb Point

**Rail
Trail**

Tomas Pond

15

**Heron Flats
Trail**

14   13

Birding Trail #1

Refuge Road

Bay Overlook

San Antonio Bay

Auto

Tour Loop →

Aransas

National

Wildlife

Refuge

THE SAND MOUNDS

Dagger Point

P

E

Refuge Road

14

Sierritos Windmill
11

to Big Tree Trail and observation tower

Birding Trail #2

hills. A trail leads directly from the Dagger Point parking area to an observation deck over the sandy beach, with a nice view of San Antonio Bay and the many waterfowl that populate it, including pelicans, gulls, ducks, geese, and spoonbills. After enjoying this view, walk back toward the parking lot and turn at the sign to the Dagger Point hiking trail (you are taking the green loop), which heads up ancient sand dunes covered with live oaks and shrubs, winding through brush and oak thickets and past dune ponds.

The sandy, narrow track is mostly shady, but at the top of the first hill you get views of the water. This loop intersects with a shorter one, and you can turn right if you want to walk out to the beach again. Otherwise, continue straight, past a swampy pond, through thick brush, and up and down the dunes. The rolling of waves and calls of birds are the only sounds on this hike. At one of the highest points of the trail, the brush opens up and offers a view of the refuge to the west.

You will eventually emerge on the road just a few yards from the parking lot. Driving south from here, the next turnoff is for Birding Trail 2, a short balloon trail toward the bay, and the next is for Big Tree Trail. The stop after that is the observation tower, which offers a panoramic view of San Antonio Bay and Mustang Lake. Then you can drive back out of the refuge the way you came in or continue on the auto tour loop, which is a total of 16 miles.

Just a short drive south from the visitors center is parking for the Heron Flats Trail, 1.4 miles through freshwater sloughs, shell ridges, oak forests, and tidal flats where you are likely to spot tricolored herons, great egrets, and other birds. However, alligators are also common along this route through wetter, lower parts of the refuge, and this presents a danger for dogs. If you decide to take your dog on this loop, follow the alligator etiquette outlined in the introduction section of this guide. The grassy and sometimes soggy trail is to your left from the parking area, through reeds and brush with freshwater ponds on one side—this is where you are likely to spot alligators—and salt flats on the other. You may notice the honking of geese flying overhead and ducks taking off and landing in the water.

After passing a series of ponds, the trail veers left and heads toward the other side of them, onto higher ground, ridges formed by oyster shells and storms, and taller brush and trees. Another observation deck affords a good view of the ponds and numerous birds. The trail surface becomes crushed shell, with a boardwalk through an open area, then

Bridget looks for alligators from the safety of a boardwalk on the Heron Flats Trail in the Aransas National Wildlife Refuge.

grass again as you enter thick trees. Oaks, redbays, and others are tangled and twisted together, with many snaking along the ground and covered in thick green moss. Vigilant hikers may spot deer or armadillos out in the broad daylight, and you are certain to encounter mosquitoes. At a trail intersection, continue straight ahead, through another open area and back to the parking lot.

55. Matagorda County Beach

Distance: 3 miles one way
Hiking time: Varies
Difficulty: Easy
High point: Sea level
Elevation gain: None
Best hiking season: Fall through spring
Regulations: Permits are required to drive on the beach. Dogs are allowed off leash on the beach but must be under the owner's control
Map: USGS Matagorda 7.5' quadrangle
Contact: Matagorda County Precinct 2 Beach Jurisdiction, 979-863-7861

Getting there: Take US Highway 59 south from Houston to Wharton, then State Highway 60 to Bay City through Wadsworth to Matagorda.

Dogs and owners alike enjoy the gentle beaches of Matagorda County.
(Photo courtesy LCRA)

Then take Farm to Market Road 2031 across the intracoastal waterway via one of the last swing bridges still in use in Texas, about 7 miles to where the road dead-ends at the beach.

Notes: There is no shade or drinking water along the beach, so prepare with sunscreen and hats for you and your dog, and carry plenty of water. Fishing is allowed from the beach and four free public piers, three on the old river channel and one on the Gulf. Tent camping is also allowed on the beach and is free. Restrooms and showers are available in the county park at the end of FM 2031.

Matagorda County Beach extends 22 miles along Matagorda Peninsula in the Gulf of Mexico, starting from where the Colorado River spills into the bay and both empty into the Gulf. The county maintains the first 3 miles of the beach, providing trash cans and keeping the surface conducive to driving. Beyond that, conditions may vary drastically. The Lower Colorado River Authority is developing a 1600-acre park and preserve near

*Hikers should avoid walking on the sea oats and other vegetation in the
dunes on Matagorda County Beach.*

the mouth of the river, called Matagorda Bay Nature Park. The park currently includes RV camping sites, kayak and walking trails, fishing piers,
picnic shelters, restrooms, and showers. The first half mile of the beach
is in the nature park and is pedestrian only, no cars allowed.

This broad, flat beach is remote enough that it does not generally
have the crowds seen on other Texas beaches, which makes for pleasant
hiking and excellent beachcombing. In addition to shells typical to the
Texas coast, you and your dog also may come across driftwood, bottles,
even old Spanish coins or fossils. The tide and waves are generally gentle
here, so it is a good place for a swim. Dunes rise at the edge of the beach,
covered with coastal grasses such as sea oats, and the coastal marshes
behind them attract a variety of birds. In fact, Matagorda County is one
of the nation's top birding spots and the number-one spot in the Audubon Society's annual Christmas bird count for more than six years—231
species and nine million individual birds in one day. The beach is within
the 15-mile radius of the bird count. Once you have traveled a mile or so

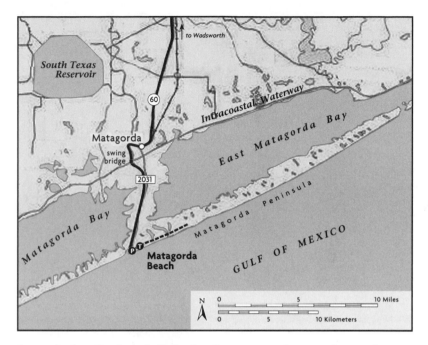

down the beach, there is little development and you and your dog can enjoy the wind, waves, and calls of gulls.

When you reach the end of the maintained portion of the beach, turn around and retrace your steps. If you feel adventuresome, you can go farther; just be careful as conditions can be unpredictable.

Trees grow in interesting ways along the Barton Creek Greenbelt, which experiences dramatic floods.

RESOURCES

The Texas Parks and Wildlife Department website, *www.tpwd.state.tx.us*, is a valuable resource for those who enjoy the outdoors in Texas. It includes information on each state park, natural area, historic site, and wildlife management area, as well as information on plants and animals found in Texas and resources on snakes, bugs, and other topics.

Find information on first aid for dogs at *www.canismajor.com/dog /fstaidk.html*.

When you travel with your buddy, find dog-friendly accommodations at *www.travelpet.com*, *www.takeyourpet.com* (low-cost membership required), or *www.petfriendly.com*.

Doggy sunglasses (including prescription ones) and sunscreen are available from *www.doggles.com*. The sunglasses (goggles, really) also provide protection from wind and debris on hikes or while riding in the car.

The Gentle Leader Headcollar provides immediate, gentle control of your dog and can transform hikes with a "sled dog" into a pleasant experience. Get more information and find where to buy one at *www.gentleleader.com*.

Basics like dog backpacks, water bowls, and first-aid kits are available from *www.planetdog.com* (travel bowls, booties, and more), *www.granitegear .com* (booties and bowls), *www.pawsuppetsupply.com* (including pooper scoopers and bags), and *www.ruffwear.com* (packs, booties, bowls, and info on selecting gear for your dog).

Just a few yards along the Hiking Trail at Palmetto State Park, trees have grown around an old wagon wheel, perhaps left behind by settlers who came to the area in the early 1800s.

INDEX

Alligators 23, 186, 189, 211, 214, 221, 223, 225
Aransas National Wildlife Refuge 223-226
Arkansas Bend Park 67-69
Austin Parks and Recreation 45, 48

Barton Creek Greenbelt 45-48
Barton Springs 45
Bastrop State Park 88-91
Bayou Trails *see Galveston Island SP*
Beebrush/Live Oak/Vireo Hill Trail 76-79
Big Slough Trail *see Brazoria National Wildlife Refuge*
Big Thicket National Preserve 195-202
Biosphere Reserve 195
Birch Creek 107–109
Bird blinds 110, 161, 163, 211
Brazoria National Wildlife Refuge 213-216
Brazos Bend State Park 191-194
Buescher State Park 93-97
Bull Creek District Park 51
Bull Creek Greenbelt 48-51

Camp Care/Cleanup 33
Canyon of the Eagles Nature Park 73-81
Cibolo Nature Center 117-120
City ordinances 26
Civilian Conservation Corps (CCC) 88, 94, 127, 171, 189
Colorado Bend State Park 138-141
Colorado River 102, 106, 138, 227
Comanche Bluff Trail 152-155
Counties 26
Crystal Beach 207-209

Dagger Point Trail *see Aransas National Wildlife Refuge*

Eagles 74, 79, 140
Echo Canyon Trail 145-148
Eisenhower Park 114-116
Elm Lake Trail *see Brazos Bend SP*

Emma Long Metropolitan Park 42-44
Enchanted Rock State Natural Area 142-148

Fawn Trail 160-163
Feet/paws 17, 19
First aid 31, 231
Flash floods 34
Fleas 20
Food 32
Forty-acre Lake Loop Trail *see Brazos Bend SP*

Galveston County 208
Galveston Island State Park 209-212
Gear 29, 231
George Bush Park 176-178
Getting in shape 17
Getting lost 33
Good Water Trail 82-88
Government Canyon State Natural Area 124-126
Grelle LCRA Recreation Area 61-64
Guadalupe River 135, 137
Guadalupe River State Park 134-138

Harris County George Bush Park *see George Bush Park*
Health concerns 17
Heartworm 19
Heat 36
Heat stroke 18
Heron Flats Trail *see Aransas National Wildlife Refuge*
Hill Country State Natural Area 148-155
Homestead Trail *see McKinney Falls SP*
Huntsville State Park 188-191
Hurricanes 35, 36

Inks Lake State Park 70-73

Lake Bastrop South Shore Park 91-93
Lake Brownwood State Park 168-171
Lake Georgetown *see Good Water Trail*
Lake Houston State Park 178-181
Lake Livingston State Park 182-185
Lake Somerville State Park 107-110

Lake Texana State Park 186-188
Lake Travis 59, 62, 65, 67, 68
Lakeside Trail 79-81
Leave No Trace 27
Lower Colorado River Authority 24, 25, 61, 64, 91, 101, 105, 227
Leon Creek Vista *see O. P. Schnabel Park*
Lightning 34
Lone Star Hiking Trail 202-206
Lost Pines Trail *see Bastrop SP*
Lost Maples State Natural Area 156-159
Lytle's Loop *see Government Canyon*

Matagorda County Beach 226-229
Matagorda Island Wildlife Management Area 219-222
McKinney Roughs Nature Park 101-107
McKinney Falls State Park 98-101
Medina River Park 120-123
Memorial Park 172-176
Mosquitoes 19
Muleshoe Bend Recreation Area 64-67
Myths about dogs 27-28

National Recreation Trail 203
Nails Creek 108, 109, 110
North River Trail *see Lake Houston SP*

Onion Creek 55, 56, 98
O. P. Schnabel Park 111-114

Pace Bend County Park 58-61
Padre Island National Seashore 216-219
Palmetto State Park 127-130, 232
Parks Pass 24
Peacock/Juniper Ridge Loops 73-76
Pecan trees 56, 71
Pedernales Falls State Park 131-134
Permits and Regulations 24
Poison ivy 23
Poop 16
Puppies 17

Repellant 19-20

Richard Moya Park 55-57
Rio Medina Trail *see Medina River Park*

Sam Houston National Forest *see Lone Star Hiking Trail*
San Antonio Parks 11, 114, 120
San Jacinto River 179, 181, 205, 206
Snakes 20-22
Socialization 15
Somerville State Park *see Lake Somerville SP*
South Shore Park *see Lake Bastrop*
South Llano River State Park 160-167
Southeast Metropolitan Park 52-55
Spicewood Springs Trail *see Colorado Bend*
Sunburn 19
Sundew Trail 195-197

Ten essentials 29-30
Texas Oak Trail *see Lake Brownwood SP*
Texas State Parks 24, 40, 231
Thunder 34
Tonkawa 83, 142
Tornadoes 35
Trail Etiquette 15-16
Travis County Parks 52, 55, 58, 67
Turkey Creek Trail *see Emma Long Metropolitan Park*

Vet check-ups 18

Water 32
Water bottles 27
Weather 34
Whooping cranes 223
Wildlife Management Area Trail 164-167
Wolf Mountain Trail *see Pedernales SP*
Woodland/Bluff Ridge Trails 104-107
Woodlands Trail 198-202

Yucca/Hill View Trails *see Eisenhower Park*

ABOUT THE AUTHOR

Melissa Gaskill and hiking buddy Max ready to tackle the Lake Somerville Trailway (photo by Collin Gaskill)

Melissa Gaskill lives in Austin with her husband and their three children. She has been writing for newspapers and magazines for more than fifteen years on a variety of topics, including travel, the outdoors, and nature, as well as health care, parenting, and family topics. She published a short story in the *Five O'Clock Shadow and Other Stories,* an anthology by Fish Publishing, Ireland. and is currently working on a book for parents of lacrosse players. She grew up on the Texas coast, spent her childhood camping and hiking all over Texas and the Southwest, and continues to enjoy the outdoors with her family. Her family has two dogs—Keeper, a Labrador retriever who would rather be hunting than hiking, and Max, a mixed-breed adopted from the animal shelter who has turned into an almost ideal hiking buddy (except for all that hair he leaves in the back of the car). Gaskill is active in her neighborhood public schools and in youth and mission work at Covenant Presbyterian Church.

THE MOUNTAINEERS, founded in 1906, is a nonprofit outdoor activity and conservation club, whose mission is "to explore, study, preserve, and enjoy the natural beauty of the outdoors. . . ." Based in Seattle, Washington, the club is now the third-largest such organization in the United States, with seven branches throughout Washington State.

The Mountaineers sponsors both classes and year-round outdoor activities in the Pacific Northwest, which include hiking, mountain climbing, ski-touring, snowshoeing, bicycling, camping, kayaking, nature study, sailing, and adventure travel. The club's conservation division supports environmental causes through educational activities, sponsoring legislation, and presenting informational programs.

All club activities are led by skilled, experienced instructors, who are dedicated to promoting safe and responsible enjoyment and preservation of the outdoors.

If you would like to participate in these organized outdoor activities or the club's programs, consider a membership in The Mountaineers. For information and an application, write or call The Mountaineers, Club Headquarters, 300 Third Avenue West, Seattle, WA 98119; 206-284-6310. You can also visit the club's website at *www.mountaineers.org* or contact The Mountaineers via email at *clubmail@mountaineers.org*.

The Mountaineers Books, an active, nonprofit publishing program of the club, produces guidebooks, instructional texts, historical works, natural history guides, and works on environmental conservation. All books produced by The Mountaineers Books fulfill the club's mission.

Send or call for our catalog of more than 500 outdoor titles:

The Mountaineers Books
1001 SW Klickitat Way, Suite 201
Seattle, WA 98134
800-553-4453
mbooks@mountaineersbooks.org
www.mountaineersbooks.org

The Mountaineers Books is proud to be a corporate sponsor of The Leave No Trace Center for Outdoor Ethics, whose mission is to promote and inspire responsible outdoor recreation through education, research, and partnerships. The Leave No Trace program is focused specifically on human-powered (nonmotorized) recreation.

Leave No Trace strives to educate visitors about the nature of their recreational impacts, as well as offer techniques to prevent and minimize such impacts. Leave No Trace is best understood as an educational and ethical program, not as a set of rules and regulations.

For more information, visit *www.LNT.org*, or call 800-332-4100.

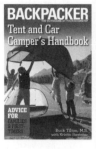

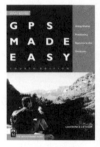

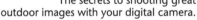